Deterrence by Diplomacy

Deterrence by Diplomacy

Anne E. Sartori

PRINCETON UNIVERSITY PRESS
PRINCETON AND OXFORD

Published by Princeton University Press, 41 William Street, Princeton, New Jersey 08540

In the United Kingdom: Princeton University Press, 3 Market Place, Woodstock, Oxfordshire OX20 1SY

Library of Congress Cataloging-in-Publication Data

Sartori, Anne E., 1966–
    Deterrence by diplomacy / Anne E. Sartori.
        p. cm.
    Includes bibliographical references and index.
    ISBN: 0-691-11699-7 (cl : alk. paper)
        1. Diplomacy. 2. Deterrence (Strategy) I. Title.

JZ1305.S37 2005
327.2—dc22   2004058694

British Library Cataloging-in-Publication Data is available

This book has been composed in Sabon type face

Printed on acid-free paper.∞

pup.princeton.edu

Printed in the United States of America

10 9 8 7 6 5 4 3 2 1

*To my husband, Jonathan Parker, and
my sons, Julian and Asher Parker-Sartori*

Contents

Preface

MOST SCHOLARS of international relations at least pay lip service to the importance of diplomacy. However, the logic of their theories implies that diplomacy contributes little to states' abilities to attain their foreign-policy goals.

The pessimists can be classified into two main stripes, though they consist of a larger number of academic subgroups. The first stripe consists of scholars who argue that the main road to foreign-policy success is power, often in the form of military strength. Some of these "realists" write that diplomacy is important, but then suggest that it is superfluous for a powerful state and ineffective for a weak one. One group argues that the United States must fight over unimportant issues to prove that it is willing to fight about important ones. A recent literature on crisis bargaining inadvertently supports the realists by suggesting that diplomacy works only if sending a message is costly. The intent of this literature is to stress the importance of domestic politics, but some read it as a prescription that states' communications occur through use of the military (which is costly) rather than through diplomacy (which is cheap).

The second stripe of pessimists consists of scholars who argue that communication among states is difficult because statespeople are human beings; they suffer from psychological biases in the ways that they interpret information, and these biases prevent communication. This argument suggests that diplomacy is even less effective than the realists had argued.

In this book, I aim to provide a new rationale for the use of diplomacy as a foreign-policy tool. I explain why states often should believe and learn from each other's diplomacy, and I provide evidence that states often do use diplomacy effectively to attain important foreign-policy goals in the course of international disputes. While I agree that military strength matters, I argue that the honest use of diplomacy is just as important to success in the international system. In doing so, I hope to contribute both to U.S. foreign policy and to scholarly debates over the causes of international crisis behavior.

Because this is a scholarly book, I use both a mathematical (game-theoretic) model and statistical evidence to make my point. But because I believe the book to have important policy implications, I try to explain the ideas and the empirical evidence in words.

I have benefited greatly during the course of this project from the counsel and support of many people. My greatest intellectual debt is to Chris

Achen, for pushing me to think extremely hard. I also am grateful to Paul Huth, Ennio Stacchetti, and William Zimmerman for helpful comments on the dissertation on which this book is based. I am grateful to Tom Christensen, Avery Goldstein, Taylor Fravel, Fred Greenstein, and Jenny Sartori for helpful comments on chapter 2, and to Adam Meirowitz, Randy Calvert, and Eduardo Castro for helpful comments on chapter 3. For help in rethinking and revising the manuscript, I particularly thank Joanne Gowa, Bob Powell, Gary Bass, Chuck Myers, Ken Schultz, Fiona McGillivray, and Ed Mansfield. I thank David Austen-Smith, Bruce Bueno de Mesquita, Bear Braumoeller, David Rousseau, Steve Durlauf, Ken Kollman, David Meyer, Bob Pahre, and Alastair Smith for useful suggestions on various portions of the manuscript. Eduardo Castro, Beth Bloodgood, Eylem Icin, Paul Martin, Min Ye, Wesley Stockard, and Todd Spiegelman provided excellent research assistance. I thank the Committee on Research in the Humanities and Social Sciences at Princeton University for funding for research assistance. I also thank CBRSS at Harvard University for the gift of a year and a collegial environment in which to finish this book. I am grateful to many audiences for insightful comments on all or parts of the manuscript: the Author-Meets-Author Conference, Christopher Browne Center for International Politics at the University of Pennsylvania, Columbia University International Politics Seminars, the Seminar of Globalization and Equity at Duke University, the Political Economy Research Workshop at Harvard University, the Applied Statistics Workshop at Harvard University, the Yale University Department of Political Science, the Rutgers University Department of Political Science, the Political Economy Interest Group of the Program for the Study of Complex Systems at the University of Michigan, the 1999 Annual Meeting of the Public Choice Society, the 1996 Annual Meeting of the American Political Science Association, the 1996 Annual Meeting of the International Studies Association, and the 1995 Junior Master Class in Formal Theory at the Merriam Laboratory for Analytic Political Research at the University of Illinois at Urbana-Champaign. Any errors in this work are my own. Portions of chapters 2 and 3 were printed in Sartori (2002); I am indebted to MIT Press Journals for permission to reprint this material here. Finally, I thank Wamiq Chowdhury for proofreading the manuscript.

I thank my family, Leo, Eva, and Jenny Sartori, Jonathan Parker, and Julian Parker-Sartori, for their constant support.

PART I

Introduction

CHAPTER 1

Introduction

THIS BOOK IS ABOUT deterrence and diplomacy. An attempt at deterrence is a counter-threat. It is a threat by one state to use military force if another state does not refrain from some undesired, threatened action. For example, a state may threaten to invade another state or to subject it to an economic blockade. The threatened state may attempt deterrence by counter-threatening to start a war if the first state goes through with the invasion or blockade.

At a casual glance, it is not clear that deterrent threats ever should succeed, because states that do not intend to fight have strong incentives to bluff. In the early 1990s, prior to NATO military intervention in the Yugoslav War, the Bush and Clinton administrations, the European Community, and the United Nations threatened to impose sanctions and then to use force to influence the behavior of Serb president Slobodan Milosevic. If the threats had worked as intended, they would have prevented the slaughter of many civilians and perhaps made NATO participation in the war unnecessary (Keesing's Contemporary Archives 1992, 1993; Silber and Little 1997). The United States and others had an incentive to claim a willingness to take actions that they were, in fact, proven unwilling to take, at least in the short run. Similarly, when Turkey threatened to invade Cyprus in June 1964, President Johnson sent a "brutal note" to deter this attack.[1] This time, deterrence worked. But Johnson, too, had an incentive to bluff if he did not intend to take action; a successful bluff would have changed Turkey's behavior in exactly the same way as a genuine threat. When states' leaders hear a threat, they must ask themselves, "Is this a bluff, or is my adversary truly willing to do what its leaders say?"

As the saying goes, talk is cheap. So why do leaders pay so much attention to each other's threats? Why does deterrence ever succeed? When is it more likely to work, and when is it more likely to fail?

In this book, I study deterrence as a form of diplomacy. Diplomacy is the use of language and other signals by one state in an attempt to convey information to another. It is a kind of communication—the use of language by representatives of one state, aimed at influencing the actions

---

[1] Under Secretary of State Ball in Lebow and Stein (1990, 362).

of one or more others. Deterrence is the use of a particular subset of language—deterrent threats—to attempt to convey the information that a state is willing to fight over a disputed issue or issues.[2] Thus, deterrent threats are a form of diplomacy.

I study deterrence in order to shed light on the question of why diplomacy so often is effective. Studying deterrence leads me to a theory of communication between states. Thinking of deterrence as a form of talk also leads to insights into why deterrence itself is effective and when and why it is likely to succeed.[3]

Many of the existing books about diplomacy are written by professional diplomats, whose studies are concerned primarily with the activities of the diplomatic corps (e.g., Nicolson 1939; de Callières 1919; Stearns 1996). Like many of those authors, I see a distinction between the making of foreign policy on the one hand, and diplomacy on the other; diplomacy concerns the implementation of foreign policy.[4] However, I would argue that diplomacy includes the work of top foreign-policy leaders as well as of members of the diplomatic corps. A nation's top foreign-policy leadership formulates and implements policy. For example, when a foreign minister announces to the press that her country is likely to join a war, she is implementing a policy (which may be broader than the decision to join the war). Such a statement never is purely policy formulation.

Deterrence is an important phenomenon in its own right. States sometimes attain their foreign-policy goals, while at other times they achieve little of what they desire. States' allies sometimes remain safe, while at others they are conquered. States sometimes themselves lose territory, at others gain. When states gain territory, this process may be peaceful, or it may involve a long and bloody war.

In order to understand the foundations of foreign-policy success and the causes of war, we must understand what leads states to try and to succeed in deterrence. To change the status quo, a state usually makes a demand of another state. If one state makes a demand accompanied by a threat and the recipient of the demand does not try deterrence, then the first state gains something and the second loses something. The most famous example of "deterrence not tried" is Britain's and France's acquiescence

---

[2] The language of international relations has evolved over the years so that the diplomatic lexicon contains both words and actions (Jervis 1970). Like words, some actions have meanings associated with them that are commonly understood by leaders. For example, moving an aircraft carrier to a troubled region is commonly understood to be a threat to use military force. Diplomacy includes speeches, conversations between presidents and premiers, the movement of troops, and the mobilization of forces. Any of these signals can be used to convey a threat to use force; it can be used for deterrence.

[3] In conceptualizing deterrence as a form of language, I especially build upon Jervis (1970).

[4] See, for example, Nicolson (1939, 15).

to Hitler's demands at Munich. If the threatened state tries to deter an attack but fails, then either the states go to war, or the aggressor gains at the expense of its foe. However, if the threatened state tries to deter an attack and succeeds, then the state that is trying to change the status quo fails to attain its goal. To understand which states get what, and when, one must study deterrence. Similarly, one must study deterrence to know what leads to its failure and to war.

Though the details of this book are about deterrence, statesmen and members of the diplomatic corps face the same credibility problem when they engage in other forms of diplomacy. Diplomacy is particularly necessary when states' interests are not perfectly aligned, when leaders have something to "work out" and often something to hide. For example, in trade, environmental, or arms control negotiations, diplomats usually have an incentive to dissemble about precisely how much their state is willing to give up; pretending to be unmovable can result in a more favorable bargain. Negotiating partners must ask, "Is this a bluff, or is my negotiating partner truly willing to walk away from the table if s/he does not get this bargain? Should I believe this promise, or does my negotiating partner have some ulterior motive for making it? Will s/he renege somewhere down the line?"

For this reason, it is not clear that diplomacy ever should be an effective tool of state. Yet leaders spend hours in conversation, and most countries employ extensive diplomatic corps. Why does diplomacy ever succeed? When is it more and less likely to work?

Talk is cheap, but it has repercussions. This book argues that states are able to use deterrence effectively precisely because it is so valuable. States often are tempted to bluff, or dissemble, but a state that is caught bluffing acquires a reputation for doing so, and opponents are less likely to believe its future communications. With less credibility, a state is less likely to get its way in future disputes. Thus, the prospect of acquiring a reputation for bluffing—and reducing the credibility of its future deterrent threats—keeps a state from bluffing except when doing so is most tempting. In other words, to maintain their ability to use deterrent threats in future disputes, state leaders often use them honestly today. They sometimes even acquiesce to opponents' demands; they do so in order to stress that they are serious on those occasions when they insist they will *not* acquiesce.

As with deterrence, states are able to use diplomacy effectively because it is so valuable. The prospect of acquiring a reputation for lying—and lessening the credibility of the state's future diplomacy—keeps statesmen and diplomats honest except when fibs are the most tempting. That is, to maintain their ability to use diplomacy in the future, representatives of states usually use it honestly.

1ation of deterrence and diplomacy that I propose in this book
ions about who gets what, and when. Contrary to much of
on international relations, my theory implies that diplomacy
tive. It also implies that deterrence is a tool for the weak, as
well as the strong. Thus, weak states, too, often can use threats to attain
their goals. While some theories of deterrence suggest that states must fight
to gain credibility for their threats, this book suggests that the honest use
of diplomacy is an alternative road to credibility.

Three Misconceptions About Diplomacy

Many scholars of international relations write that diplomacy works.
Nevertheless, I see the implications of the international-relations literature
as largely pessimistic about the prospects for effective diplomacy. This
pessimism comes in part from three misconceptions: (1) that the effectiveness of a threat is equivalent to the communicator's military strength
and/or its resolve, or willingness to fight; (2) that "cheap talk" is ineffective; and (3) that disbelief requires a psychological explanation. While
I am not the first to argue against these ideas, they nevertheless remain
prevalent. This section discusses them in turn.

The Effectiveness of the Communication Is Equivalent to a Communicator's Capabilities and/or Resolve

The first misconception—that the effectiveness of a threat is equivalent
to the communicator's military strength and/or its resolve—arises from a
school of thought called *deterrence theory* and from the broader, related
school referred to as *realism*. Both of these schools of thought emphasize
the importance of military force and/or power. Each consists of a large
number of loosely related works.[5] Here, I merely discuss a few fairly
common themes that are relevant to my arguments; I do not attempt to
summarize the work of all scholars in these literatures.

According to what is often called "rational" deterrence theory, state
leaders are rational actors who, in a crisis, try to decide whether or not
war is in their interest.[6] They do so, according to the theory, by calculating

---

[5] Those outside academe may know realism as the theory espoused by politicians like
Henry Kissinger who believe in the importance of power politics (Kissinger 1994). For
academic discussions of realism, see Doyle (1997, Part I, 41–204); Vasquez (1998). On
deterrence theory, see, for example, Leng and Gochman (1984); Huth and Russett (1984);
Huth (1988); Huth, Gelpi, and Bennett (1993). Also see Fearon (1992, chapter 2) for a nice
review of the deterrence literature.

[6] I discuss works that apply psychological models to study deterrence later.

the expected costs and benefits of going to war and of remaining at peace. A crisis begins when one state (a "challenger") threatens to use force to obtain something of value to another (a "defender"). The challenger may wish to obtain something concrete, such as a piece of territory, or something abstract, such as a change in the defender's policy. The goal of deterrence as a strategy is to convince a challenging state to back down from its threats by counter-threatening the use of force (issuing a deterrent threat). If it works, the counter-threat indicates to the challenger that the costs of using force will be high and/or the benefits will be low. Deterrent threats may be threats to impose pain on the challenging state if it proceeds to attack, or they may be threats to deny the challenger its goals by fighting.[7]

A central question among scholars of deterrence is that of when deterrent threats will be credible. "Credible," of course, means "believable"; deterrence theorists are concerned with when an adversary will believe a state's threats to fight.[8] This question is crucial because a deterrent threat only affects the challenging state's assessment of the costs and benefits of an attack insofar as the challenger believes the threats.

A common theme in the literature is that crisis behavior and credibility are heavily influenced by two factors: the military capabilities and resolve of the states involved in the crisis.[9] Resolve is an amorphous concept, used in different ways by different scholars; Fearon (1992, 69) defines the composite well as the "willingness to use force." Scholars of deterrence differ about what creates a willingness to use force; some argue that it stems from having greater interests at stake in the dispute (Snyder and Diesing 1977; George and Smoke 1974; Maxwell 1968), while others maintain that it is a dispositional quality, perhaps a willingness to take risks (Kahn 1965; Schelling 1966).[10] Though "capabilities" and "resolve" are separate terms in the deterrence literature, few deterrence theorists would deny that capabilities also affect crises by influencing states' willingness to use force.

---

[7] Some scholars draw a strong line between deterrence and defense, arguing that deterrence is only about punishment and not about denial. However, as Morgan (1977, 21, 30) and Snyder (1961, 3–15) explain, deterrence can consist of threats to defend. A successful defense both removes the benefits of an attack and imposes costs on the attacker.

[8] See Huth (1988, 33–55) for an excellent discussion of the logic of credibility in deterrence theory.

[9] Leng and Gochman (1984) and Huth (1988) focus on the bargaining behavior of the disputants, and Bueno de Mesquita (1981) and Bueno de Mesquita and Lalman (1986) focus on the role of alliances. However, even when deterrence theorists focus on factors other than capabilities and resolve, they often also argue that one or both of these factors is important in determining crisis behavior.

[10] If resolve is the willingness to use force, a state's interest in the dispute and/or its willingness to take risks influence, but do not determine, its resolve, according to these arguments. Most scholars see resolve as determined by a combination of factors.

Why do deterrence theorists believe that capabilities and resolve increase a state's credibility? If deterrence fails, a state with relatively stronger or more technically advanced military forces is better able to deny its adversary its goals and/or to impose greater costs on the adversary (Huth 1988, 35–9). At the same time, a militarily stronger state is more willing to defend, since it is more likely to prevail in war. Since militarily stronger states are more willing and more able to follow through on their threats, their adversaries are more likely to believe their deterrent threats and to believe that the threatened action actually will harm them and/or deny them their goals. Similarly, more resolved states are more likely to fight if necessary, and to fight hard enough to win. Their adversaries also are more likely to believe their threats to fight and to believe that the threatened action will harm them and/or deny them their goals. Thus, states are more likely to attain their goals after issuing deterrent threats if they are stronger and/or more resolute. Of course, they also are more likely to attain their goals *without* deterrent threats if they are stronger and/or more resolute, since others know that strong, more resolute states are more likely to win wars if push comes to shove.

Realist scholars as a group are less concerned with crisis behavior than are deterrence theorists, and more concerned with macro events, such as the prevalence of war in the international system. However, as in deterrence theory, one of the unifying ideas in realism is that power and/or military force is extremely important in deciding the course of international events (Doyle 1997, 43).[11] Many realists argue that a more powerful state's diplomacy will be more effective than that of a less powerful one; for example, Hans Morgenthau argues, "[D]iplomacy must determine its objectives in light of the power actually and potentially available for the pursuit of these objectives" (Morgenthau 1967, 539–40).[12]

In sum, most deterrence theorists and many realists argue that deterrence and/or diplomacy are effective tools of state. *However, while these scholars pay lip service to the importance of diplomacy, many of their arguments suggest that diplomacy is essentially irrelevant.* According to their arguments, credibility comes from might or resolve. Diplomacy is superfluous for a powerful or resolute state, which will attain its goals anyway; it is ineffective for a weak or irresolute state, which will not attain its goals with or without diplomacy.

---

[11] Realists mean many different things when they discuss "power"; a discussion of what constitutes power to realists is beyond the scope of this book.

[12] Vasquez (1998, 36) argues that Morgenthau's work "was the single most important vehicle for establishing the dominance of the realist paradigm within the field."

| 1. Challenger has initial beliefs about whether or not defender will fight | | 2. Defender's threat, if effective, provides new information, changes challenger's beliefs | | 3. Challenger has new beliefs about whether or not defender will fight |

FIGURE 1.1. A Chronology of the Challenger's Beliefs

The arguments about credibility and diplomacy that I have just reviewed contain a core of truth but confuse three ideas. In a dispute, the challenger begins with some assessment of the defender's willingness to use force to prevent the challenger's desired change in the status quo (figure 1.1). As the dispute progresses, the challenger's assessment may change or stay the same. The defender's deterrent threat, if effective, provides new information that changes the challenger's beliefs about the defender's willingness to use force, or to take some other threatened action. After hearing the defender's threat, the challenger then has new beliefs about the defender's willingness to use force over the disputed issue.

An adversary's initial assessment of a state's willingness to fight depends upon the military balance and on what is known about a state's resolve, for reasons that the deterrence theorists suggest. However, the concept of so much concern to deterrence theorists—the credibility, or believability, of the threat—is the listener's assessment of the threatener's willingness to fight *after* hearing the threat, box number 3 in figure 1.1. Deterrence theory does not adequately explain how a state can change its adversary's beliefs about its capabilities and resolve during the course of a dispute.[13] Thus, in arguing that diplomacy is primarily the instrument of power or resolve, realists and deterrence theorists effectively suggest that the adversary's initial assessment of the situation determines the effectiveness of the threat.

In a dispute, both a state initially believed to be irresolute (less willing to fight) and one initially believed to be resolute (more willing) wish to

[13] Fearon (1992, chapter 2) makes a similar argument. Powell (1990) and Huth (1988) are two exceptions. Powell explains the credibility of nuclear threats in a situation of mutually assured destruction (MAD). In contrast to many deterrence works, he concludes that the state with the greatest resolve need not prevail (177–8). Huth (41–2) argues that the local balance of forces, near to the site of conflict, is the most important in influencing deterrence, and that a state can change the adversary's beliefs by actually changing that balance during an international crisis.

The present work shares the focus of a recent literature that is concerned with how states convey information over the course of a dispute (e.g., Morrow 1989; Powell 1990; Fearon 1997; Bueno de Mesquita, Morrow, and Zorick 1997; Smith 1998b; Schultz 2001). It differs from this literature in examining each dispute in the context of a state's ongoing international relations, as I discuss later, and from much of this literature in explaining credibility as a result of international rather than domestic factors.

convince an adversary that the adversary's initial assessment of the situation is mistaken; the threatener is *more resolved than previously thought*. For example, in the Yugoslav crisis discussed earlier, the United States had an incentive to appear more resolute—whether it was, in fact, quite resolute, or whether it was bluffing in an attempt to provide safety for Milosevic's victims at little cost. There is no a priori reason to believe that the state initially believed to be resolute will be more effective in convincing an adversary that the adversary has underestimated its resolve, that it is even more resolute than the adversary at first believed.

Political realists and deterrence theorists are correct when they argue that power and resolve affect the course of disputes. They are wrong to infer that a more powerful state's diplomacy therefore must be more effective in changing an adversary's mind or that it must be more credible. Understanding the circumstances under which threats will be credible and deterrence will be effective requires a theory that explains the value-added of diplomacy. This book aims to provide such a theory.

Cheap Talk Is Ineffective

It is the current (though perhaps passing) trend among scholars of international politics to claim that talk is a waste of time. More technically, some scholars believe that signals must be costly to convey information and that "cheap talk" is ineffective.[14]

The international-relations arguments about the ineffectiveness of cheap talk draw on a literature on costly signals in economics. In the economics literature, a "costly signal" is one that has a direct (and negative) effect on the sender's well-being. A cheap-talk signal may have eventual negative consequences, but the message itself is costless to send. For example, if one must pay $1,000 to make a speech, that speech is a costly signal. If one simply holds a press conference or sends a diplomatic note, then the speech is cheap talk.[15]

If signals must be costly, then diplomacy is a monumental waste of time. Diplomacy is the epitome of cheap talk; it includes speeches, communiqués, and diplomatic notes.

The widespread dismissal of cheap talk as ineffective in international relations is the consequence, probably unintended, of part of a literature in international relations on "audience costs." The point of the audience-costs literature is to emphasize the impact of domestic politics on international behavior; scholars in this school argue that the existence of domestic audiences allows states to signal their intentions. Some

---

[14] But see Kydd (1992); Smith (1998a); Morrow (1994); Ramsay (2003).

[15] However, see the discussion on the audience-costs literature in chapter 3.

works in this vein even argue that cheap talk can work (Smith 1998a; Ramsay 2003). However, as I discuss in more depth in chapter 3, part of the literature gives the impression that signals must be costly to convey information, so that cheap talk does not work.[16]

In actuality, the dismissal of cheap talk has neither a theoretical nor an empirical basis. While the economics literature does show the effectiveness of costly signals (see, e.g., Spence 1974), a related literature in economics shows that signals that carry no cost often convey information (Crawford and Sobel 1982; Farrell and Gibbons 1989). In common usage, the phrase cheap talk refers to talk that probably is unreliable. Yet every person in human society knows that talk can be a very useful means of communication. Speakers choose their words carefully when it matters, because even cheap talk can have repercussions.

In international relations, talk that technically is "cheap"—diplomacy—can be very powerful. When states do try to deter actions by means of diplomatic threats, they often succeed in persuading their challengers to back down. For example, the Anglo-Russian Treaty of 1942 specified that both Britain and Russia were to withdraw their troops from Iran by March 1946. When the Soviets threatened to remain in parts of Iran after that date, the U.S. chargé d'affaires in Moscow delivered a diplomatic note to the Soviet government calling for the withdrawal of troops from Iran, and the Soviet Union withdrew its troops.[17]

This book reconceptualizes diplomacy and deterrence as cheap talk. While deterrence theory focuses on the possession of military capabilities and the resolve to use them, I focus on threats as a form of communication. In the work that follows, I show that states can use even cheap diplomacy to change their adversaries' minds in international crises.

Disbelief Requires a Psychological Explanation

One important critique of realist views of international relations comes from scholars applying ideas from the field of psychology (e.g., Jervis 1976; Lebow 1981). These scholars argue that states are led by human beings who misperceive incoming information to such an extent that communication and deterrence are difficult or impossible. For this reason, these critics are at least as pessimistic as the realists about the prospects for diplomatic solutions to international conflict.

[16] It is not uncommon to hear scholars make the point that cheap talk is ineffective in conversation and to attribute this claim to the audience-costs literature.

[17] While Lebow and Stein classify the Iran case as "not a deterrence encounter," it was a situation in which the Soviets threatened and the United States issued a diplomatic protest that tried to deter the threatened action. See Lebow and Stein (1990, 357–8); Keesing's Contemporary Archives (1946, 7757, 7865); Herzig (1995).

As psychological theorists emphasize, the success of language is by no means a given in the context of international disputes. However, most difficulties that arise in communication require no psychological explanation (Fearon 1992, chapter 2). Communication is difficult because states have incentives to lie about their willingness to use force. A United States that was not willing to protect "safe areas" in Yugoslavia had an incentive to threaten to do so, since bluffs sometimes succeed. As long as states sometimes bluff, it is perfectly rational for threatened states sometimes to disbelieve the threats they hear.

This book explains why states often do believe each other's diplomacy. Nevertheless, while my explanation focuses on states' incentives to use threats honestly, it also explains why states sometimes do give in to temptations to bluff. Since diplomacy is not 100 percent honest, it also is not 100 percent credible, nor is it always effective. As I explain later in the book, diplomacy works, but not all the time or under all circumstances.

How Can a State Communicate That an Adversary Has Misjudged Its Resolve?

In 1968, the United States acquiesced to the Soviet invasion of Czechoslovakia. This decision was not a high point of moral policy making, but any threats over Czechoslovakia would have been bluffs. U.S. leaders seemed to realize the benefits of honesty; when Russian ambassador Anatoly Dobrynin told President Johnson that U.S. interests were not affected by the Soviet action in Czechoslovakia, "[i]n response he was told that U.S. interests are involved in Berlin where we are committed to prevent the city being overrun by the Russians."[18] Johnson's words reveal that he saw a difference between Czechoslovakia, where he was honestly admitting that there were no strong U.S. interests, and Berlin, where he was threatening and prepared to go to war.

In contrast, Russian leaders bluffed in the early Balkan conflicts, and these bluffs may have harmed the effectiveness of their subsequent diplomacy. In the conflict of 1908–9, Russia backed down from its initial support for Serbia, leading Serbia to recognize Austria-Hungary's annexation of Bosnia-Herzegovina.[19] When the Austro-Serbian conflict flared up again in 1912, Russia bluffed again, accepting Albanian independence when it became clear that Germany would support Austria-Hungary. [20]

---

[18] Summary Notes of the 590th Meeting of the National Security Council, in Department of State (1996, 274).

[19] Albertini (1952, 190–300). This case is classified by Snyder and Diesing (1977, 137) as a "Called-Bluff" adversary crisis.

[20] Helmreich (1938).

Russia's threats in 1914 then were ineffective. Based on the issues, one might have expected Russia's threats to be *more* credible in 1914. The issue in 1914 was the invasion of a Slavic state by Austria; based on estimates of Russia's interests, other states should have believed that Russia was likely to fight. Yet this was not so.[21]

These examples illustrate two facts. First, states sometimes honestly acquiesce to each other's demands, despite incentives to bluff. Second, when a state is caught bluffing, it acquires a reputation for doing so, and such a reputation hinders its ability to use diplomacy in the near future.

As I argued earlier, one purpose of diplomacy is to communicate to an adversary that a state is more resolved to fight over disputed issues than the adversary believes to be the case. Earlier, I noted that the effectiveness of diplomacy is puzzling because states' representatives have incentives to bluff, or dissemble. This book explains the effectiveness of diplomacy as, in part, the result of another strong incentive—the incentive to use diplomacy honestly in order to avoid a reputation for bluffing. Because much of diplomacy is honest, states are able to learn from each other's words.

Leaders often believe each other's deterrent threats because these threats are often—though not always—honest. States tend to be honest when they are willing to fight; they have no incentive to hide that fact. But, like the United States in the Czechoslovakian crisis of 1968, states sometimes also honestly acknowledge that they are not prepared to fight, even when that means acquiescing to unwanted change. States do bluff, but they bluff only rarely. Like Russia at the beginning of the last century, they acquire reputations for bluffing when they bluff and are caught. When a state is caught bluffing, others are unlikely to believe its diplomacy soon thereafter. The state then cannot use diplomacy honestly to convince another to back down; nor can it bluff successfully. It is less likely to attain its goals. The desire to avoid a reputation for bluffing, or to maintain a reputation for honesty, induces states to use their diplomacy honestly much of the time.

Reputations for honesty play a key role in explaining the success of diplomacy. When a state has a reputation for honesty, it is better able to use diplomacy successfully to communicate that it is more resolved than

---

[21] In a 1914 letter to the German Ambassador to Britain, the German Foreign Secretary writes, "The more boldness Austria displays the more strongly we support her, the more likely is Russia to keep quiet. There is certain to be some blustering in St. Petersburg, but at bottom Russia is not now ready to strike" (in Turner 1970, 85).

One cannot know if Germany would have been deterrable in 1914 if German leaders had believed the Russian threats. What is known is that German leaders did not believe the threats and that Russia was not bluffing. Once the Russians became convinced that diplomacy was failing, they mobilized for war. A few days later, Germany mobilized in turn and declared war on Russia (Turner 1970).

an adversary previously had believed to be the case. Since other work on deterrence discusses reputations for having resolve, it is worth emphasizing here that reputations for honesty differ from those reputations.[22] A state acquires a reputation for honesty when others observe it acting honestly. This happens when a state actually acts honestly, as well as when it bluffs and is not caught. A state can act honestly in two ways. Under some circumstances, it honestly can claim to be resolute about a particular issue (i.e., threaten, and then fight if deterrence fails). Alternatively, it honestly can acknowledge that it is *irresolute*; it can acquiesce to an adversary's demands.[23]

Unlike many theories of international relations, this book leads to optimistic conclusions about diplomacy. In demonstrating why states often are able to use deterrence, a type of diplomacy, effectively, I suggest an explanation for why diplomacy works more generally. Like deterrent threats, diplomacy is likely to work because it is so valuable; states that misrepresent their positions may be caught, and may suffer decreased ability to communicate in the near future.

This explanation of diplomacy—elaborated later in the book—also provides clues as to when diplomacy and deterrence are more or less likely to be successful. A state's diplomacy is less likely to be effective when the state recently has been caught bluffing, more likely to change an adversary's mind when the state recently has used diplomacy honestly or engaged in a successful bluff.

While traditional deterrence theory suggests that a state should fight or strengthen its military to increase its credibility, my work shows that there is another path: honest acquiescence, too, can increase a state's ability to use diplomacy in the future, by letting an opponent know that the state will threaten only when it really does intend to fight. Moreover, both powerful states and weak ones can increase the effectiveness of their future diplomacy by using their diplomacy honestly today. Thus, diplomacy is a tool for the weak as well as the strong.

OVERVIEW OF THE BOOK

In the remainder of this book, I first present my argument as to why and when diplomacy works, then offer evidence in support of that argument.

Chapter 2 uses a case of failed deterrence to illustrate a central feature of my explanation: reputations for bluffing hurt a state's credibility and

---

[22] For an introduction to the idea of reputations for resolve, see Huth (1997). I discuss these reputations further in chapter 3.

[23] This argument builds upon Jervis's seminal work on communication between states. See Jervis (1970, 78–80).

lessen the effectiveness of its diplomacy. This chapter examines China's attempt to deter UN forces from crossing the 38th parallel during the Korean War. The case is a fascinating one because the Chinese made numerous and varied attempts at deterrence and the United States probably did not want to fight China, but China's attempt at deterrence failed anyway. This study details how U.S. officials dismissed China's threats as bluffs, and argues that China's difficulties in using diplomacy stemmed, in part, from recent, unfulfilled threats vis-à-vis Taiwan. Because they came in the context of these threats, China's threats to enter the Korean War were less credible. Because the United States did not believe China's threats, China had to go to war in order to attain its goal—keeping U.S. forces away from its border.

Chapter 3 formalizes my explanation of successful deterrence and diplomacy in a game-theoretic model of repeated international disputes. Using the model, I prove that "cheap-talk" threats often are effective in deterring an attack because states wish to maintain their reputations for using diplomacy honestly.

Chapter 4 presents statistical evidence that this theory helps to explain actual disputes and crises. I analyze data from more than 1,300 international crises, and many additional cases in which states did not threaten the use of force. I find that these disputes, on average, progress in ways implied by my explanation of diplomacy. In particular, reputations for honesty help to make diplomacy effective. A state with a reputation for honesty is more likely to succeed in deterring an attack. As the theory suggests, this is because its diplomacy is, in fact, more likely to be honest. The fact that these patterns arise in the data, as the theory predicts, helps to confirm the usefulness of the theory.

The theory uncovers reputations for honesty or for bluffing as an important variable for helping to explain states' behavior. Specifically, it explains why these reputations are critical for understanding the escalation of existing international disputes. In chapter 5, I speculate that this variable also affects states' decisions to become involved in disputes in the first place and I investigate this speculation empirically. I also explore the impact of the military balance on dispute escalation.

Chapter 6 summarizes the findings of the book. It also returns to a discussion of how this theory expands our understanding of diplomacy more generally. Finally, I discuss ideas for future research.

Current scholarship in international relations encourages the dangerous view that diplomacy is superfluous, does not work, or can be made to work only through the use of force or other costly signals. This book shows that diplomacy does work—though, like any other tool of state, it is not a sure thing.

PART II

How Bluffs Can Hurt a State's Diplomacy, and Honesty Provides the Ability to Communicate

CHAPTER 2

The Failure of Chinese Diplomacy, 1950

> The Chinese people absolutely will not tolerate foreign aggression nor will they supinely tolerate seeing their neighbors savagely invaded by the imperialists.
>
> —Chinese Foreign Minister Zhou En-lai one week before the U.S. First Cavalry Division crossed the 38th parallel into North Korea, and about two weeks before large numbers of Chinese communist "volunteers" crossed into North Korea, enlarging the Korean War and pitting Chinese against U.S. troops.[1]

AT THE END OF World War II, the United States proposed, and the Soviet Union accepted, a division of Korea into two occupation zones. The Japanese, who had occupied Korea, were to surrender to the Soviets north of the 38th parallel, and to the United States south of that line. At the time of the Japanese surrender on September 2, 1945, Soviet forces were in Korea, as far south as the parallel, and U.S. forces would not arrive for another few days. After unsuccessful negotiations, the division of the country became further entrenched with elections in the south in May 1948, creating the Republic of Korea (ROK), and with the establishment of the Democratic People's Republic of Korea (DPRK) in the north in August of the same year (Rees 1964, 9–10). Both Korean governments claimed sovereignty over the whole peninsula. After helping to strengthen the South Korean army, the United States withdrew its last troops from Korea in June 1949, leaving its precise military commitment to South Korea unclear (Stueck 1995).

One year after the last U.S. troops withdrew from Korea, on June 24, 1950, North Korean leaders sent over 100,000 soldiers over the border into South Korea with the idea of reunifying Korea by force under their control.[2] The next day, the UN Security Council passed a resolution proposed by the United States, calling for a cease-fire, for North Korean

---

[1] Report to the National Committee of the People's Political Consultative Conference commemorating the first anniversary of the founding of the People's Republic of China, September 30, 1950, as quoted in Department of State (1976b, 852).

[2] For an interesting but controversial argument that the South may have provoked the war, see Cumings (1990, 568–621).

withdrawal to the 38th Parallel, and for UN member states to aid in the execution of the resolution (Rees 1964, 21–2). On June 27, the UN Security Council voted in favor of another American resolution recommending that member states "furnish such assistance to the Republic of Korea as may be necessary to repel the armed attack and to restore the international peace and security in the area" (as quoted in Rees 1964, 24). This resolution paved the way for an effort by the United Nations to repel the North Korean forces. Many countries participated in the UN effort in some way. In addition to the United States, fifty-three of the fifty-nine UN members in June 1950 eventually approved the second resolution, forty countries offered aid, and fifteen sent troops. However, the resistance to North Korea's invasion was heavily American. The UN forces were under the command of U.S. General Douglas MacArthur; at the end of 1951, over half of the total forces under UN command in Korea were American (Rees 1964, 21–33). For this reason, I concentrate in this study on decision making in the United States.

Initially, the North Koreans routed the South Korean forces and the few American troops that had arrived in Korea to assist them. However, the tide of the war began to turn in favor of the UN side after the UN forces' successful amphibious landing at Inchon on September 15, 1950, behind North Korean lines (Stueck 1995, 47–8, 85–7). As early as July 1950, Truman indicated that sending troops across the border into North Korea was a possibility, after the successful UN landing at Inchon, members of Congress increased their pressure on the administration to do so (Foot 1985, 68–9).

In November of that year, China entered the Korean War. Chinese leaders tried almost every diplomatic method available to communicate that China would enter the war if U.S. or UN forces crossed the 38th parallel into North Korea, but President Truman and most members of his administration nevertheless maintained that China would not intervene. Had the United States believed the threats, it might have refrained from crossing the parallel. Since neither China nor the United States appears to have wanted to fight the other, successful signaling on China's part might have avoided a tragedy.[3]

The case of China's failed diplomacy during the Korean War shows the difficulties of diplomacy and its enormous potential benefits. The chapter will argue that China's many and varied threats were clear in meaning. U.S. leaders understood the warnings and knew that China was capable of intervening. China's deterrence failure most likely was due to the

---

[3] Some scholars argue that the United States would have crossed the parallel even if U.S. decision makers had believed the Chinese threats, and others argue that the Chinese would have intervened even if U.S. forces had stayed below the parallel. I discuss these issues later.

perception on the part of the United States that China was bluffing. This perception, in turn, was due in part to the fact that China's threats to enter the Korean War came in the context of a series of unfulfilled threats regarding Taiwan. The episode illustrates how being seen as bluffing leads to expectations that a state will not carry out its later threats. Such expectations hinder the state's ability to use diplomacy in the immediate future, an ability that can be extremely valuable.

Sources

This chapter relies heavily on information contained in the vast secondary literature in English on the Korean War. It does so because the purpose of this chapter is to make a new argument, rather than to uncover new pieces of information.[4] The interpretation of almost every aspect of the Korean War is controversial; I flag the most-relevant controversies.[5] Later in the chapter, when I discuss China's threats to Taiwan, I rely more upon Chinese-language sources, both primary and secondary, because the literature in English is more sparse.[6] The use of sources released by the Chinese government is, in general, somewhat problematic; as William Cohen argues, the government "remains in power and is not committed to a systematic opening of its archives" (Zhang and Chen 1996, xviiii). In addition, there have been some reports of secondary sources in Chinese that were discovered to be plagiarized versions of other Chinese-language articles.[7] However, I am aware of no claims that the available Chinese-language sources are fabricated. Moreover, I report information from U.S. documents and news articles that confirms the tenor of the information I obtain from the Chinese sources. Thus, the information that I report from the Chinese sources probably is accurate but incomplete.

---

[4] The gist of the chapter's central argument, that China's ability to deter the United States from crossing the 38th parallel was hindered by a reputation for bluffing, is not new; other scholars, for example Lichterman (1963, 590) and Huth (1988), have made similar arguments.

[5] The Korean War case raises numerous interesting questions beyond those discussed here. For example: What were the origins of the Korean War? Why did the United States exclude Korea from its defense perimeter? What was the extent of Chinese and Soviet involvement in the planning of the war? Millett (1997); Foot (1991, 1996); and Munro-Leighton (1992) provide helpful introductions to the literature. A number of political-science works discuss some aspect of the war, including George and Smoke (1989); Neustadt (1990); Whiting (1960); Schelling (1966); Zelman (1967); Huth (1988); Christensen (1992); Jervis (1976); LeBow (1981); Orme (1987); and Halperin (1963).

[6] I am indebted to Min Ye for research assistance using Chinese sources, for translating portions of the sources for me, and for the transliterations from the Chinese that I use in this chapter.

[7] Taylor Fravel, personal communication, 2002.

Like all politicians, Chinese leaders are likely to have used their statements strategically. The strategic use of statements is not a problem for this study, however, since the study rests on an assumption that all statements are strategic.

The Chinese Attempt at Deterrence

In the summer and fall of 1950, China's leaders made a concerted diplomatic effort to deter U.S. and UN troops from crossing the 38th parallel into North Korea. The United States was threatening to send troops across the border into North Korea, and China counter-threatened to enter the war if it did so.

China's diplomatic attempts included both military signals and verbal threats.[8] The Chinese engaged in large-scale movements of troops toward the Chinese–North Korean border. Between mid-May, just over a month prior to the start of the war, and mid-July, China redeployed 60,000 troops, placing "180,000 of Peking's best troops within one month's march of the Korean battle front," and even closer to North Korea (Whiting 1960). The redeployment paused from July till mid-September, and resumed after the Inchon landing of September 15; approximately 320,000 Chinese troops were in Manchuria, close to North Korea, in mid-October 1950 (Zelman 1967, 5). China did not try to hide these troop deployments, suggesting that they were meant, in part, as a warning to the United States (Whiting 1960, 106, 111).

While the troop movements could have been routine, statements made verbally by the Chinese leadership in the summer and fall of 1950 indicated otherwise. China's leaders and semi-official publications began to warn of Chinese intervention in late August. The Chinese had two reasons to believe the likelihood of UN forces crossing the parallel to be greater in mid- to late August than they had before. First, the military balance shifted in favor of the UN side during the second week of August, in part due to the fact that U.S. troops had had time to make their way to Korea. Second, U.S. leaders began to talk more about unifying Korea. On August 10, the U.S. delegate to the United Nations made a speech that referred to unification; President Truman mentioned the issue publicly at the end of the month (Stueck 2002, 96).

As I describe later, U.S. leaders dismissed the threats as bluffs; Truman and Secretary of State Acheson later justified this error by arguing that the threats came through an unreliable messenger, the Indian Ambassador to China, K. M. Panikkar, and/or that they came around the time of

[8] On China's attempts at deterrence, see, especially, Zelman (1967).

a UN vote on Korea. These arguments are implausible for several reasons, including the variety of sources issuing the threats, the timing of the threats, and, as I discuss later, Truman's and Acheson's own discussions of the threats in their memoirs.[9] The verbal threats took three forms: public statements by China's leaders, threats in articles in newspapers and journals closely linked to the government, and statements that were relayed by Panikkar. They began in late August, long before the UN vote in question, and continued through early October, after South Korean forces crossed the parallel on October 1. The Chinese continued to threaten after South Korean forces crossed the parallel because their threats were aimed at the Americans, as I discuss later.

On August 26, the journal associated with the Ministry of Foreign Affairs, *World Knowledge* (*Shi Jie Zhi Shi*), gave the first serious warning:

> The barbarous action of American imperialism and its hangers-on in invading Korea not only menaces peace in Asia and the world in general but seriously threatens the security of China in particular. The Chinese people cannot allow such aggressive acts of American imperialism in Korea. To settle the Korean question peacefully, first the opinions of the Korean people and next the opinions of the Chinese people must be heard. . . .
>
> No Asian affairs can be solved without the participation of the Chinese people. It is impossible to solve the Korean problem without the participation of its closest neighbor, China . . . North Korea's friends are our friends. North Korea's defense is our defense. North Korea's victory is our victory.[10]

Whiting notes that the Chinese deleted the last two lines when Radio Beijing broadcast the article to North America, suggesting that China did not yet want to make such a strong, clear threat. However, even without those lines, the article stated clearly that China considered the Korean conflict to affect it directly: the action "seriously threaten[ed] the security of China in particular." The warning that "[t]he Chinese people [could not] allow such aggressive acts" also threatened action, albeit vaguely.

The threats became stronger in late September and stronger still in October. On September 22, China admitted sending aid to the North Koreans, and it threatened to send more. A Ministry of Foreign Affairs spokesman said that China "will always stand on the side of the Korean

---

[9] Twomey (2004, 177–9) also challenges the argument that the United States disbelieved China's threats because the Chinese used Panikkar as a messenger. He argues instead that differences in the two states' theories of victory are key to understanding the failure of the Chinese signals.

[10] From World Knowledge (Shi Jie Zhi Shi), 22, no. 8 (August 26, 1950), as quoted in Whiting (1960, 84–5). China had been engaged in domestic propaganda against the United States for some time, and the propaganda had become more negative in tone beginning with the "Resist American Invasion of Taiwan and Korea" campaign of July–August 1950.

people."[11] The next day, an article appeared in the Chinese communist party newspaper *Ren Min Ri Bao* (*People's Daily*), querying, "Is it not just for us to support our friend and neighbor against our enemy?" (Whiting 1960, 106). On September 25, the Acting Chief of Staff of the People's Liberation Army, General Nie Rong-Zhen, told Indian ambassador Panikkar that China "did not intend to sit back with folded hands and let the Americans come up to their border" (Panikkar 1955, 108).

On September 30, in an official speech to the Central People's Government Council, Chinese Foreign Minister Zhou made the statement quoted at the beginning of this chapter: "The Chinese people absolutely will not tolerate foreign aggression nor will they supinely tolerate seeing their neighbors savagely invaded by the imperialists."[12] On October 2, the day after South Korean forces crossed the parallel, Zhou called Panikkar to a midnight meeting and told him, "The South Koreans did not matter but American intrusion into North Korea would encounter Chinese resistance" (Panikkar 1955, 110).[13] The United States was told of Panikkar's conversations with Nie and Zhou; the Chinese could not converse directly with the U.S. ambassador instead of Panikkar because there was no such ambassador.[14]

What were China's goals in attempting deterrence, and later in intervening? This subject is one of some controversy in the literature. Allan Whiting's classic book on the war (1960) emphasizes China's desire to protect its security, and more recent works (e.g., Christensen 1996, Stueck 2002, 107–8) agree that security was an important consideration. The prospect of U.S. troops in North Korea raised at least two security concerns for the Chinese. First, a noncommunist Taiwan was the status quo; a successful UN invasion of North Korea would thus require that China maintain strong defenses on two borders. Moreover,

---

[11] Radio Beijing in English, as quoted in Whiting (1960, 105).

[12] Though this speech was not published until the November 1950 issue of *China Monthly Review*, the Consul General of Hong Kong reported the jist of it to U.S. Secretary of State Acheson in telegrams dated October 2 and 5, 1950. See Department of State (1976b, 852) for the telegrams.

[13] The Chinese minutes of the meeting report that Zhou told Panikkar, "The American troops are attempting to cross the 38th parallel and to expand the war. If the American troops actually do that, we cannot sit by idly without making a response. We will intervene" (Zhang and Chen 1996, 164).

[14] President Truman notes in his memoirs, "On October 3 the State Department received a number of messages which all reported the same thing: The Chinese Communists were threatening to enter the Korean conflict. Chou En-lai, now the Foreign Minister of the Chinese Communist regime, had called in the Indian Ambassador to Peiping, K. M. Panikkar, and had told him that if United Nations forces crossed the 38th parallel China would send in troops to help the North Koreans. However, this action would not be taken if only South Koreans crossed the 38th parallel" (1956, 361–2).

keeping forces on their northern border "would be fiscally expensive and also politically dangerous, because the American presence near North China would embolden domestic counterrevolutionaries while the dual-purpose military forces needed to combat them were occupied on the border" (Christensen 1996, 156). Second, Chinese leaders saw a U.S. decision to cross the parallel as a sign of U.S. aggressiveness; Mao cabled Zhou that "not to have intervened . . . would have meant that 'the reactionaries at home and abroad would be swollen with arrogance when the enemy troops press on toward the Yalu River [the border between North Korea and China].' "[15]

The theory that China intervened out of concern for its security is consistent with the timing of Chinese intervention; China did not actively participate in the North Korean invasion of South Korea, but rather entered the war only when North Korean independence was in danger. As Thomas Christensen has documented, Mao did not make the decision to enter the war in force until the crossing appeared imminent:

> Various data from early October suggests that the American crossing of the 38th parallel on October 7, 1950, was the triggering event that convinced Mao to enter the war in force. Mao's initial decision to enter the war (October 2) was made the day after MacArthur called for the surrender of all North Korean forces on both sides of the parallel. Mao gave his initial orders to form the Chinese People's Volunteers on October 8, the day after American troops began crossing the parallel. On the same day he informed [North Korean leader] Kim Il-sung of China's intention to enter the war. (Christensen 1992, 136; text in brackets added).

Finally, as I discussed earlier, China's leaders publicly stated that they would intervene only if the United States were to cross into North Korea.

Over the past ten to fifteen years, scholars have published several new works on the Korean War that make use of newly available sources (Chinese and Russian sources, in particular). Jian Chen's book merits special attention here because it maintains that the Chinese did not attempt deterrence sincerely at any point in the war. Rather, Chen argues, Mao and his comrades were inclined to go to war with the United States, "aim[ing] to win a glorious victory by driving the Americans off the Korean peninsula" (Chen 1994, 3).[16] According to Chen, the Chinese had such strong interests at stake that "there was little possibility that China's entrance into the Korean War could have been averted" (1994, 5).

---

[15] Mao in Gaddis (1995, 80). Christensen also argues that the U.S. decision to cross the parallel convinced Mao that the United States had aggressive intentions toward China (e.g., 1992, 136).

[16] Gaddis (1995, 80–81) also stresses Mao's predilection toward war.

Chen explains China's threats as a feint, designed to buy time so that China could ready itself for war.

However, other recent works agree with Whiting that China intervened out of concern for its security, including Christensen (1992, 128), and also Goncharov, Lewis, and Xue (1993, chapters 5 and 6), who document Mao's reluctance to fight the United States.[17] Moreover, Chen himself notes that, as of September 24, 1950, the Chinese leadership had not made the final decision to enter the war (1994, 163–4).

If Chen is right and the Chinese were bent on war, then the Korean War case is not one of failed deterrence. Either way, the central question of this chapter remains: why were China's threats not credible?

China's diplomacy indicated that it considered keeping U.S. and UN forces south of the parallel so important that it was prepared to fight a war over this issue. China's leaders did not simply assume that the United States recognized the extent of their interests. On the contrary, China's leaders sent a plethora of signals. An "unusual consistency and lack of 'noise' characterized Peking's efforts to signal its intentions" (George and Smoke 1974, 188). China engaged in a "massive military redeployment" (Whiting 1960, 111), and its verbal threats were as blunt as saying that "American intrusion into North Korea would encounter Chinese resistance" (Panikkar 1955, 110). The timing of the threats contributed further to the message: they began in the summer of 1950 but became more numerous and more urgent in tone in late August after U.S. leaders began to talk publicly about crossing the parallel. If such diplomatic means had been successful in preventing the UN action, China would have attained an important goal at almost no cost.

THE U.S. DISMISSAL OF CHINA'S THREATS AS BLUFFS

The United States dismissed China's threats as bluffs. In documents from the period, many U.S. leaders (and diplomats from other countries in the UN coalition) stated that despite the threats, they did not believe that the Chinese would intervene.[18]

Secretary of State Acheson was one of the many who dismissed China's threats. Of Zhou's October 3 warnings through Panikkar, he wrote, "Chou's words were a warning, not to be disregarded, but, on the other

---

[17] See, for example, pages 174–5.

[18] That the United States dismissed the Chinese threats is one of few points on which there is widespread agreement in the literature on the Korean War. Only a few U.S. officials and analysts expressed strong concerns about Chinese intervention; see Donovan (1982, 217); and Foot (1985, 79–80).

hand, not an authoritative statement of policy" (Acheson 1969, 453).[19] At a meeting on October 4,

> [t]he Secretary pointed out that the Chinese Communists were themselves tak-ing no risk in as much as their private talks to the Indian Ambassador could be disavowed...and if they wanted to take part in the "poker game" they would have to put more on the table than they had up to the present. ... In the Secre-tary's opinion the only proper course to take was a firm and courageous one and we should not be unduly frightened at what was probably a Chinese Communist bluff." (Memorandum of Conversation by Mr. John M. Allison of the U.S. Del-egation to the UN General Assembly, in Department of State (1976b, 868–9)

MacArthur, too, argued that the Chinese would not intervene. In a famous meeting on Wake Island on October 15, 1950, he told the pres-ident that the Chinese would not attack (Truman 1956, 365). Partway through the war, MacArthur was relieved of his command and Congress held an unusual set of hearings into the military situation in the Far East and into the circumstances surrounding his relief.[20] At these hearings, MacArthur mentioned a November Central Intelligence Agency report that "said that they felt that there was little chance of any major inter-vention on the part of the Chinese forces" (U.S. Congress Senate 1951, 18). He also noted that his forces in the field were deployed on "the basis of the enemy that existed" (the North Koreans) without considering the impact of a large number of Chinese forces.[21]

Many diplomats used the word "bluff" explicitly when referring at the time to the Chinese threats of intervention. For example, the U.S. ambassador to the Soviet Union telegrammed that it "appear[ed] probable [that the] Chinese Communists . . . have taken [a] strong line since Inchon landing hoping [to] bluff UN on 38th parallel issue" (Ambassador Kirk, telegram of September 29, 1950, in Department of State 1976b, 820). A memorandum by the Director of the Office of Chinese Affairs (Clubb) on August 17, 1950, stated, "[i]f Peiping in some of its threatening statements may be trying to bluff us, it is nevertheless not yet safe to assume that the USSR has played all of its cards respecting Korea" (Department of State 1976b, 796).

---

[19] Like Truman, Acheson argues that China's credibility was influenced by the upcoming UN vote.

[20] The hearings by the Joint Senate Foreign Relations and Armed Services Committees, commonly known as the "MacArthur Hearings," were held in May through June 1951. See Rees (1964, chapter 15) for a discussion.

[21] MacArthur also maintained that the disposition would have been the same had he known of the Chinese attack (U.S. Congress Senate 1951, 19). The relevant point for my argument, however, is that he was so skeptical about Chinese threats to intervene that he doubted their veracity even after he began to see evidence of intervention.

Leaders make the same point in after-the-fact accounts. Of course, politicians have an incentive to portray themselves favorably for the historical record. In their memoirs and other accounts, both Truman and Acheson tried to justify their disbelief of the threats by blaming the messenger and the timing of the threats. As I discussed earlier, these justifications do not make sense in light of the varied sources and drawn-out timing of the threats.

Moreover, read carefully, Truman and Acheson's own accounts suggest that though they did not believe that the Chinese would take the threatened action, they understood the content of the threats. For example, Truman's *Memoirs* state:

> [T]he problem that arose in connection with these reports was that Mr. Panikkar had in the past played the game of the Chinese Communists fairly regularly, so that his statement could not be taken as that of an impartial observer. It might very well be no more than a relay of Communist propaganda. There was also then pending in the Political and Security Committee of the General Assembly of the United Nations a resolution recommending that all appropriate steps be taken to insure stability throughout all of Korea. This resolution, if adopted, would be a clear authorization for the United Nations commander to operate in North Korea. The key vote on the resolution was due the following day, and it appeared quite likely that Chou En-lai's "message" was a bald attempt to blackmail the United Nations by threats of intervention in Korea. (Truman 1956, 362)

In this passage, Truman justifies his dismissal of the threats on the grounds that they came through Panikkar, an unreliable messenger, and were aimed at influencing a UN vote. The passage indicates, however, that he understood that the threats originated with the Chinese and that their purpose was to deter UN forces from crossing the parallel. First, Truman claims that the Chinese threats lacked credibility because the United States mistrusted the Indian ambassador. (He writes that Panikkar was sympathetic to the Chinese Communists.) However, if Truman had not understood that the threats originated with the Chinese, he would not have called the warnings "a relay of Communist propaganda." Second, Truman maintains that the threats were aimed at influencing a vote in the United Nations, not at deterring U.S. forces from crossing the parallel. However, since the resolution in question would authorize UN operations in North Korea, Truman's words indicate that he understood the threats to be aimed at stopping UN action in North Korea.

Perhaps the most remarkable aspect of the U.S. disbelief of China's threats was the date to which it persisted. While the historical record is somewhat unclear on this subject, the U.S. government remained unconvinced that the Chinese were engaged in a large-scale offensive even after MacArthur's forces encountered Chinese troops. On November 6, General MacArthur reported to the Joint Chiefs that "[m]en and material in large force are pouring across all bridges over the Yalu from Manchuria. This movement not only jeopardizes but threatens the ultimate distribution of the forces under my command" (as reported by Truman 1956, 375). The Chinese admitted on November 7 that they had sent troops into North Korea. At the MacArthur hearings, however, the general noted that "[i]n November, our Central Intelligence Agency, here, had said that they felt there was little chance of any major intervention on the part of the Chinese forces" (U.S. Congress Senate 1951, 18). Similarly, in his testimony at the hearings, Acheson stated that on November 24, "it was said that there was not available evidence for a conclusion as to whether the Chinese Communists were committed to a full-scale offensive effort" (U.S. Congress Senate 1951, 1834). This was true despite the fact that Acheson, Secretary of Defense Marshall, and others had access to a November 8 CIA report which "estimated that combined Chinese and North Korean ground forces on the peninsula could compel their UN counterparts to withdraw to 'defensive positions further south'" (Stueck 2002, 114). At the same time, Acheson writes in his memoirs that, "[d]uring the depressive period of November 6–8 the Chiefs of Staff informed him [MacArthur] that his 'objective' (the destruction of the North Korean Army) stated in the September 27 directive might have to be re-examined as the eventuality mentioned in it—the entry of Communist China into the war—seemed to have occurred" (1969, 465).

Any U.S. skepticism in middle-to-late November is partly explained by the fact that the Chinese disengaged from the fighting between November 7 and November 26 (Zelman 1967, 12). In fact, it appears that China was no longer trying to deter the U.S. action by this time; after UN forces crossed the parallel, Chinese actions were dictated by warfighting strategy (Christensen 1992, 1996). In particular, Mao wanted the Americans to underestimate China's military capabilities so that they would overextend themselves (Christensen 1996, 170–73).

Nevertheless, China's temporary disengagement fails to explain why U.S. leaders were not convinced by the Chinese warnings in September and October, when the Chinese were moving troops and making threats. It also fails to explain any remaining skepticism in early November, before the Chinese temporarily disengaged. China's leaders had stated that they would not tolerate UN forces in North Korea, and U.S. leaders knew of the presence of Chinese troops in North Korea. Even after this evidence of intervention, however, U.S. leaders did not acknowledge that the Chinese planned a large-scale military action in Korea.

Believing that China would stay out of the war, U.S. troops crossed the 38th parallel into North Korea on October 7, 1950. The Chinese secretly began to move troops into North Korea approximately a week later, and U.S. forces encountered them in early November (Whiting 1960).

WOULD THE UNITED STATES AND CHINA HAVE FOUGHT IF CHINA'S THREATS HAD BEEN CREDIBLE?

The world never will know, of course, if the United States and China would have avoided fighting each other if U.S. leaders had believed the Chinese threats. Anticommunism was extremely popular in the United States, and both political parties perceived political advantage in advocating a strong response to the North Korean invasion (Foot 1985, 69–70). There was widespread support for crossing the parallel both in the Truman administration and in Congress.

However, the historical record suggests that the administration did not want to fight China and would have kept U.S. forces south of the parallel to keep China out of the war. MacArthur's last instructions from the Joint Chiefs of Staff prior to October 7, when U.S. troops first crossed the parallel, stated:

> Your military objective is the destruction of the North Korean Armed Forces. In attaining this objective, you are authorized to conduct military operations, including amphibious and airborne landings or ground operations north of the 38th Parallel in Korea, *provided that at the time of such operations there has been no entry into North Korea by major Soviet or Chinese Communist Forces, no announcement of intended entry, nor a threat to counter our operations militarily in North Korea.* (Department of State 1976b, 781; italics added)[22]

The fact that the Joint Chiefs instructed MacArthur to stay out if there was "announcement of intended entry" of Chinese forces suggests that the United States did not want to fight China and planned to cross into North Korea only if it believed China to be staying out. The document also told MacArthur not to halt air and naval operations in North Korea, once started, "merely because the presence of Soviet or Chinese

---

[22] These instructions were based on NSC 81/1, which stated, "The United Nations Commander should undertake no ground operations north of the 38th parallel in the event of the occupation of North Korea by Soviet or Chinese Communist forces . . . If the Soviet Union or the Chinese Communists should announce in advance their intention to reoccupy North Korea and give warning, either explicitly or implicitly, that their forces should not be attacked . . . Action north of the 38th parallel should not be initiated or continued, and if any U.N. forces are already North of the parallel they should prepare to withdraw pending further directives from Washington (Department of State 1976b, 716–17). The directive was approved by Truman on September 27. See also Department of State (1976b, 785, 792–3); Foot (1985, 74); Acheson (1969, 453).

Communist troops is detected in a target area," but rather to notify Washington in the event that the Soviets or the Chinese announced an intention to occupy North Korea. On balance, however, MacArthur's instructions indicate that President Truman and the Joint Chiefs of Staff would have favored keeping U.S. and UN troops below the parallel if they had believed that sending the troops north of the parallel would lead to Chinese intervention.[23]

Some scholars argue that MacArthur was eager to proceed into North Korea regardless of whether or not he believed China's threats, and that Truman ultimately agreed with his view (e.g., Neustadt 1990, 114; George and Smoke 1976, 191). The former seems likely; MacArthur favored an aggressive military posture (Rees 1964, chapter 15; Stueck 2002, 113). Moreover, most members of the Truman administration became proponents of the idea of "limited rollback," the idea that America might not only contain but also, in a limited way, roll back communism; "By June 1950, Acheson was one of the few Truman administration officials who remained opposed to rollback" (Cumings 1990, 709). However, while Truman was tempted to try to reunify Korea under South Korean leadership, and faced domestic pressure to do so (Foot 1985; Stueck 2002, 115), his memoirs and MacArthur's instructions indicate that he was unwilling to fight the Chinese to attain this goal. On the contrary, he and many others in his administration were tempted to attempt reunification precisely because they did not believe the Chinese threats. In the face of likely Chinese intervention, as his instructions to MacArthur indicate, Truman would have been likely to resist MacArthur's wishes and domestic pressures. He also would have been advised to refrain from crossing the parallel by his other advisers (whom he trusted more than MacArthur); statements by U.S. officials indicate that most of the leadership did not want to fight China. As late as October 23, 1950, General Bradley, chairman of the Joint Chiefs of Staff, said at a joint meeting of the U.S. and U.K. Chiefs of Staff, "We all agree that if the Chinese Communists come into Korea, we get out" (as quoted in Schnabel and Watson 1979, 263).[24]

---

[23] Some scholars (e.g., Christensen 1992, 131) argue that the warnings that the Chinese issued after September 27 were ineffective because Truman had already authorized General MacArthur's crossing of the parallel. This argument is contradicted by the instructions that I discuss in this paragraph, which authorize the crossing only on the condition that the Chinese had not intervened or announced their intention to do so.

While later instructions permitted ground operations in the face of Chinese intervention, such instructions were issued only after the United States had already crossed the parallel (Lichterman 1963, 596).

[24] According to Acheson, MacArthur later claimed that he had been given wide latitude to cross the parallel, though others in the administration have disputed this interpretation.

Thus, if U.S. leaders had believed the threats, UN and U.S. forces might well have stayed below the parallel.[25] As I discussed earlier, the available evidence suggests that the Chinese did not intend to enter the war unless the United States and/or the United Nations crossed the parallel. Moreover, Christensen argues that China would have had great difficulty attacking U.S. forces if those forces had stopped south of the parallel; to do so, the Chinese would have needed Soviet material support, and the Soviets would have been highly unlikely to provide such support (Christensen 1996, 158). Thus, it is quite likely that U.S. disbelief of China's threats led the two states into a war that neither wanted. In any case, the question remains: Why did U.S. leaders not believe China's threats?

WHY DID THE UNITED STATES DISMISS CHINA'S THREATS AS BLUFFS?

U.S. leaders began the war believing that China would not intervene for two reasons: the military balance favored the UN side, and U.S. policy makers did not perceive important Chinese interests to be at stake in Korea. However, neither the balance of forces nor the initial beliefs of U.S. leaders explains why China's words did not convince the Americans that they were wrong.

Even with the existing balance of forces (which favored the United States), U.S. leaders felt a need to evaluate China's intentions; they did

---

MacArthur cited as evidence a for his "eyes only" telegram from General Marshall, then secretary of defense, saying "We want you to feel unhampered tactically and strategically to proceed north of the 38th parallel" (Marshall in Acheson 1969, 453). In his memoirs, Acheson disputes MacArthur's account, however: "[I]t is inconceivable that General Marshall should have arrogated to himself authority to give General MacArthur dispensation to violate instructions from the Joint Chiefs of Staff approved by the President and MacArthur's own plan of operations also approved by the President and himself that very day" (Acheson 1969, 453–4). While memoirs are by their nature after-the-fact accounts, Bradley's memoirs also dispute MacArthur's account; he writes, "News dispatches quoted Walker [Walton Walker, tactical commander of the UN forces in Korea] as stating he would halt at the 38th parallel, presumably to await permission from the UN to cross. This was an awkward development inasmuch as our UN diplomats were then attempting to get the UN resolution through without a specific vote on crossing the 38th parallel. Accordingly, I conferred with Marshall on September 29 and together we composed the following message" (Bradley and Blair 1983, 566). In other words, Marshall's message was intended only to convey the information that Walker's action should not be conditioned on new UN approval, not to broaden MacArthur's latitude to cross the parallel in the event of Chinese intervention.

Cumings (1990, 713) argues that most of the opposition to rollback came after the fact. However, much of the support for rollback was predicated on the assumption that the Chinese would not enter the war.

[25] Of course, it is possible that Truman would have ordered MacArthur to stay below the parallel and that MacArthur would have disobeyed.

not take for granted that China would refrain from intervention because of the military situation. Asked by Senator McMahon if MacArthur had intelligence to the effect that China would intervene "if we went to the Yalu," U.S. Army Chief of Staff General J. Lawton Collins answered, "I wouldn't say necessarily that it was a likelihood Senator, but it certainly would represent a capability" (U.S. Congress Senate 1951, 1235). Similarly, Chairman of the Joint Chiefs of Staff Bradley remarked, "We had no intelligence that they were going to enter the war. We had the intelligence that they were concentrating in Manchuria. You can only then consider their capabilities. They had the capability of intervening in the war" (U.S. Congress Senate 1951, 759).

U.S. leaders drew a distinction between China's capabilities and its intentions, and they concluded that its intentions mattered more. The view seems to have been fairly widespread in the military that the Chinese were able to intervene, despite their disadvantage, but would not do so.[26]

The reason that the Chinese would not intervene, U.S. leaders said, was that they had no important interests at stake in Korea. The United States did not see a security benefit to the Chinese of entering the war, because "the Administration believed that Peking really thought the same way it did, and saw that a serious threat to China did not exist" (Rees 1964, 113). Acheson listed the "lack of real advantage to China itself of coming in" as one of the reasons he believed that the Chinese would not enter the war (U.S. Congress Senate 1951, 2000). He also noted that China was preoccupied with domestic policy.

The military balance and U.S. beliefs about China's lack of interest in Korea explain China's need for diplomacy. The United States had evaluated the situation and decided that Chinese intervention would be disadvantageous to the Chinese themselves, and it was the task of China's diplomacy to communicate to the United States that its assessment was wrong.

However, China's need for diplomacy and the failure of its diplomacy are two separate matters. Why did the U.S. assessment of China's intentions fail to change in the face of the extensive Chinese threats, and even in the face of actual Chinese intervention? In other words, why did U.S. leaders not learn?

China's Reputation for Bluffing

Chinese leaders were unable to convince the United States of their intentions in part because Chinese diplomacy had been discredited by a series

---

[26] However, MacArthur based his argument that the Chinese would stay out of the war on U.S. military superiority (Truman 1956, 373).

of unfulfilled threats over Taiwan: these encouraged the United States to dismiss the threats relating to Korea.

The late 1940s marked the beginning of the Cold War, in Asia as well as elsewhere. The Communist forces defeated the Nationalists in China and proclaimed the People's Republic of China in 1949. The Nationalist forces retreated to a few offshore islands, primarily Taiwan. In early 1950, the U.S. government was more preoccupied with Communist Chinese threats against the Nationalist government than with Korea (Stueck 1995, 30). When the Korean War started, one of President Truman's first actions was to order the U.S. Seventh Fleet to prevent all military action in the Taiwan Strait.

The credibility of China's diplomacy at the start of the Korean War was hindered by the fact that it came in the context of a series of unfulfilled threats over Taiwan. The Chinese Communists had threatened Taiwan repeatedly during 1949–50, before and after taking power, and U.S. leaders were aware of that fact.[27]

The Chinese Communists began threatening to "liberate" Taiwan at least as early as March 1949. For example, on March 15, the Xinhua News Agency, a semi-official publication of the Chinese Communist Party (CCP), published an article entitled, "Chinese People Must Liberate Taiwan" ("Zhongguo renmin yiding yao jiefang Taiwan") (Tang and Xu 2001, 1531). In January through June 1950, the Third Division of the People's Liberation Army repeatedly claimed in print that its most important tasks included liberating Taiwan (Tang and Xu 2001). In February through April 1949, the Central CCP repeatedly directed party members that "liberating Taiwan is the most important task of the CCP" (Tang and Xu 2001, 1536).

The Chinese threats against Taiwan continued after the North Korean attack on South Korea. On June 28, 1950, four days after the attack, Chinese Foreign Minister Zhou declared that Taiwan was part of China's territory, and that China had to liberate it (Tang and Xu 2001, 1538). China's leaders designated July 17–24, 1950 to be "National Campaign Week against United States Aggression"; this campaign featured, among others, the slogans, "Intensify our work, consolidate our force, defend world peace with actual deeds," and "Intensify our preparation for the liberation of Taiwan—our own territory" (Levi 1953, 296–7). After President Truman ordered the U.S. Seventh Fleet to the Taiwan Strait on June 27, Chinese Foreign Minister Zhou called the move "armed aggression against the territory of China in total violation of the United Nations charter." Zhou also promised that China would "liberate Taiwan" despite the U.S. action (Whiting 1960, 58). On September 4, 1950, a

---

[27] The People's Republic of China was established on October 1, 1949.

People's Daily news column was devoted to the idea of liberating Taiwan (People's Liberation Army Central Command 1993, 750).

Although the United States probably was not aware of every threat, there is evidence that it was aware of the general nature of the threats. For example, in January 1950, the Consul General of Shanghai (McConaughy) sent a telegram to the U.S. Secretary of State reporting:

> Dramatic crescendo of publicity and preparations demonstrating new regime's irrevocable determination to "liberate" Taiwan has been a major feature of this political scene recent months. With each easy mainland conquest by PLA narrowing down remaining field toward Taiwan, Gino's [Chiang Kai-Shek's] last lair, build-up of confident expectations, publicized comments, economic pressures and stage-setting operations for its "certain conquest" has increased in scale and tempo.

> By late summer press was already alive with talk re need winning island. . . .

> Within recent weeks virtually every important Chinese Communist pronouncement has declared, with increasing stress and irrevocable commitment tone, the necessity and certainty of taking island. Liberation Taiwan has, in fact, been publicly announced as nation's paramount immediate mission on which PLA's and new regime's reputation and entire resources are staked. (Department of State 1976a, 265–7)[28]

China did not invade Taiwan, though it did attack other offshore islands. Thus, at the time of the Korean War, China had not fulfilled its threats to invade Taiwan.

Moreover, some of China's threats appear to have contained explicit time frames, and China did not take the threatened action by the threatened time. For example, Mao seems to have backed down from a self-imposed September 1, 1950, deadline for attacking Taiwan. During the fall of 1950, when China was issuing some of these threats, one U.S. observer wrote:

> Of course, no one, with the possible exception of our intelligence people, who naturally aren't talking, knows whether Mao will really attempt to take Formosa. Earlier this summer, he declared that he would do so by the first of September. His demand yesterday that the United Nations order our Navy to leave the waters around the island suggests that he probably plans to let that deadline pass, by a few days at least . . . It is conceivable that he has made his demand in order to provide himself with an excuse for giving up the whole

---

[28] During the first summer of the Korean War, numerous stories about China's threats appeared in U.S. newspapers. For example, see Lieberman (1950a, 1950b), Barrett (1950); Hamilton (1950).

adventure, but it is just as conceivable that he means business and will try to deliver. (Rovere 1950, 54)

While I have not found other direct evidence of deadlines, Mao himself expressed concern about having set them. In a memorandum dated September 29, 1950, he wrote:

> Please check whether or not in our past pronouncements we have ever contemplated attacking Taiwan in 1950. It is said that the New Year proclamation of this year mentioned something about attacking Taiwan within this year. Is this true? Please note that from now on we will only speak about our intentions of attacking Taiwan and Tibet, but say nothing about the timing of the attacks. (Zhang and Chen 1996, 160)[29]

In sum, China not only threatened many times in 1949–50 to "liberate" Taiwan; it appears to have set deadlines that it did not meet. The failure to meet self-imposed deadlines for an invasion probably contributed to a perception in the United States that China's threats were bluffs.

The U.S. reaction to the threats was mixed. U.S. decision makers expressed worry about a possible Chinese invasion (see, e.g., Goncharov, Lewis, and Xue 1993, 156; Foot 1985, 38–54). Moreover, in March 1950, the CIA argued that the internal political situation in Taiwan was so precarious that "an invasion could be expected to precipitate a quick collapse."[30] At the same time, several scholars have argued that China's unfulfilled threats over Taiwan contributed to its lack of credibility over Korea. As one author writes, "it was difficult for our policy-makers to perceive that the public threats, even though they were confirmed by intelligence reports, carried any more weight than the numerous other threats made by the Chinese Reds against the 'American imperialists' for their activities in Formosa and other parts of the Far East" (Lichterman 1963, 590). In a 1972 interview, Secretary of the Army Frank Pace said:

> You've got to remember that the Red Chinese had been threatening throughout the period. General Ridgway merely emphasizes that they threatened at that time, but this was not something that started at that time. Quite frankly, I guess it's a case of crying "wolf" that often. I do not believe that at that time anybody seriously believed that the Red Chinese were going to enter the war. (Interview by Jerry N. Hess in Harry S Truman Presidential Oral History Collection 1990, February 17, 1972)

---

[29] A *People's Daily* editorial of January 1, 1950 states that one of the main tasks facing China in 1950 is to liberate Taiwan (*People's Daily* 1950). This may or may not be the New Year proclamation Mao had in mind. See also Goncharov, Lewis, and Xue (1993, 158) on the subject of deadlines.

[30] CIA ORE 7-50, "Probable Developments in Taiwan," March 20, 1950, Copy No. 1 For the President of the United States, as quoted in Finkelstein (1992, 296).

In other words, according to Pace, U.S. leaders saw China's threats to enter the Korean War as additional instances of "crying wolf."[31]

Were the Chinese actually bluffing over Taiwan? China was planning an invasion; in August 1949, Mao replied to one of his commanders, "It is correct for you to take active preparations for an offensive aimed at Taiwan" (Mao in He 2003, 76). China also engaged in a campaign against several other offshore islands, and was successful in taking some of them. However, Mao postponed his plans to attack Taiwan itself several times. In October 1949, military defeats on the islands of Jinmen and Dengbu impressed China's leadership with the difficulties of offshore operations and Mao postponed the invasion in order to increase military preparedness (He 2003, 78). In May 1950, China successfully invaded the island of Hainan, which contained a substantial number of Guomindang (Chinese Nationalist) troops. However, the GMD was able to withdraw more than 70,000 troops to Taiwan before the PLA could destroy them, thus increasing the strength of GMD forces on Taiwan itself; this event again led China to revise upward its assessment of the military requirements of invading Taiwan (He 2003, 82–3). Mao once more postponed the invasion after Truman ordered the U.S. Seventh Fleet to the Taiwan Strait on June 27, 1950, at the start of the war (He 2003, 78, 87). In August 1950, China postponed the invasion until 1952, and the plans for 1952 were uncertain. The Central Military Commission (CMC) wrote, "Whether [we will] attack Taiwan in 1952 will be decided by the situation."[32] At the end of September, Mao "banned the use of slogans promising liberation by a definite date from the National Day celebration" (Goncharov, Lewis, and Xue 1993, 158).

What does it mean to bluff? In the language of deterrence theory, China was a challenger vis-à-vis Taiwan. The question, then, is about the definition of a bluff by a challenger, a state that threatens to use force to change the status quo. A state could choose to engage in a surprise attack, to attack without first threatening to do so. When a state chooses to issue threats (becoming a challenger), it does so in part to solicit information

---

[31] On China's reputation for bluffing, see also Rovere and Schlesinger (1951, 149); Lindsay (1955, 17); Zelman (1967, 16–17); Huth (1988, 144); and Schnabel (1992). Pace's is the only direct quotation that I have found of a U.S. official discrediting China's threats because of its past bluffs. However, the quotation from Rovere in the text above also suggests that this concern was at least somewhat in the public eye. Rovere and Schlesinger (1951, 148) also argue that Panikkar was disbelieved as a messenger because he had relayed too many Chinese threats in the past that had turned out to be bluffs. United Press Correspondent Jack E. James also argues that North Korea had a reputation for bluffing (Paige 1968, 83).

[32] CMC to Chen Yi, August 11, 1950, *Zhonggong Zhongyang wenjian huibian* (A collection of CCP Central Committee documents [internal version]) as quoted in He (2003, 88).

about the threatened state's or states' (defender's or defenders') willing-ness to use force to defend the status quo. Sometimes, the defender is unwilling to fight and the challenger's threats result in the desired change without the challenger being required to fight (or even to make clear if it was willing to fight). If the defender issues a counter-threat, then the chal-lenger must run a risk of war if it proceeds. If a defender's deterrent threat persuades a challenger to change its plans, the challenger is shown to be unwilling to use force to change the status quo—that is, to be willing to fight only if it is clear that there will be no resistance. Thus, if a defender's deterrent threat convinces a challenger not to attack, the challenger is shown to be bluffing.

In the Taiwan case, the threatened parties (or "defenders," in the lingo of deterrence theory) included the United States as well as Taiwan, because the United States had at times indicated an interest in Taiwan. That the Chinese saw the Americans as possible defenders is supported by the fact that the Chinese were concerned with assessing the likely response of the United States to an invasion (He 2003, 79–80). In January 1950, Su Yu, the lead planner of the Taiwan invasion, stated in reports to two confer-ences on military affairs that he did not believe the United States would send troops to protect Taiwan, though it might send weaponry (He 2003, 80). However, the movement of the Seventh Fleet to the Taiwan Strait at the start of the Korean War signaled that the United States was more willing to defend Taiwan than the Chinese had previously believed.[33] It was after the United States moved the Seventh Fleet to the Strait that China postponed the invasion indefinitely; insofar as China backed down because the United States moved the Seventh Fleet to the Strait, it did so because the United States called its bluff.[34]

It is unclear at what point a threat that an adversary has not acted upon becomes a bluff, and at what point the threat is perceived as a bluff. If a state has not yet followed through upon a threat, it still might do so in the future. As I discussed earlier, China postponed the invasion at least twice due to reassessments of its military requirements, before finally postponing it indefinitely in response to Truman's decision to move the Seventh Fleet. China was revealed to be bluffing (in the sense of being unwilling to invade if it would face U.S. resistance) by its response to

[33] A discussion of U.S. policy about Taiwan is beyond the scope of this chapter. See He (2003) and particularly Finkelstein (1992). The movement of the Seventh Fleet to Taiwan was intended to keep the Nationalists from attacking China, in addition to vice versa.

[34] The decision to postpone the invasion indefinitely was the result of many factors; these included the need to concentrate forces on two fronts due to the war in addition to the presence of the Seventh Fleet in the Strait (Goncharov, Lewis, and Xue 1993, 158). Insofar as China's reversal was due to factors other than the prospect of U.S. and Nationalist Chinese resistance, then China was not bluffing.

the Seventh Fleet. Its earlier postponements of the invasion are in the gray area. Absent the U.S. movement of the Seventh Fleet, China might well have followed through on its threats eventually, but its series of postponements may nevertheless have made its threats appear to be bluffs.

In the rest of this book, I refer to the "reputation for bluffing" that China acquired from its actions over Taiwan prior to the Korean War. What I mean by this is the pattern of behavior and beliefs that I have just discussed. China had not followed through on many of its threats against Taiwan and the United States by the time of the Korean War. China's threats to intervene in the Korean War came in the context of this long series of unfulfilled threats. Mao expressed worry about having set and missed deadlines for invading Taiwan. While China's reputation is not a complete explanation for its failed diplomacy, China's record of threatening and not following through was one of the reasons why its threats to intervene in the Korean War were not more credible.

The UN Vote, Panikkar, and Groupthink

The fact that the other proposed explanations are weak makes China's reputation for bluffing a more convincing explanation for the lack of credibility of the Chinese threats to enter the Korean War. Scholars and policy makers have proposed a number of reasons for the communication failure. In addition to China's lack of capabilities and interest in Korea, these include the timing of the threats prior to a crucial UN vote, the fact that some of them were relayed through the mistrusted Indian government, and groupthink on the part of U.S. leaders.[35]

The explanations that focus on Indian Ambassador Panikkar as a messenger are unsatisfying for a variety of reasons. As I discussed earlier, the choice of Panikkar as a messenger is a poor explanation because the threats came from a variety of Chinese government sources and he relayed only a few of them.[36] That the Chinese were trying to influence the UN vote is a poor explanation because many of the threats substantially predated the vote in question. Moreover, Truman's memoirs do not support

---

[35] George and Smoke (1974, 191) argue that the Truman administration engaged in "wishful thinking," ignoring China's warnings because it wanted to unify Korea under South Korean control. In other words, administration members were "irrational," subject to psychological biases in the way in which they processed information. This book argues that there is a rational explanation for the administration's disbelief: China had a reputation for bluffing, and states with such reputations are, in fact, likely to bluff again. They do not always bluff, however. When they are not bluffing, their lack of credibility can increase the likelihood of unwanted war, as this chapter illustrates.

[36] Christensen (1992, 131–2) argues that the United States not only mistrusted Panikkar but also questioned Zhou's authority.

his own theory; his description of the situation suggests that he understood the context of the warnings and that they came from the Chinese. Acheson's memoirs yield a similar picture. Finally, the Indian channels theory is suspect because India was not simply a communist stooge; "Indian proposals at the UN had fallen considerably short of [Soviet Delegate Jacob] Malik's position, while Delhi's relations with Peking became increasingly strained as the PRC made clear its determination to 'liberate' Tibet" (Whiting 1960, 110).

Groupthink is an insufficient explanation because President Truman, Acheson, and others had major disagreements with General MacArthur. Janis argues, "The mutual support for risk-taking, it seems to me, was part of a more general pattern of concurrence-seeking behavior, which also fosters uncritical acceptance of stereotypes of out-groups and a sense of unanimity about the wisdom and morality of past decisions."[37] Yet the U.S. conduct of the Korean War also involved behavior that cannot be explained as concurrence-seeking: Truman and others disagreed strongly with some of MacArthur's opinions, statements, and actions, and ultimately MacArthur was dismissed as Commander-in-Chief of the Unified (UN) Command.[38] Rather than "groupthink" in this crisis, there was substantial disagreement—but almost no disagreement over whether or not the Chinese were bluffing.[39]

As previously noted, many scholars argue that General MacArthur wanted to cross into North Korea whether or not China was going to enter the Korean War. That debate is interesting, but the crucial question here is whether or not MacArthur and other top leaders believed the Chinese threats, not what MacArthur or the United States would have done if U.S. leaders had believed them. Their statements indicate that they did not believe the threats.

In fact, it is remarkable that in an administration replete with power struggles over the conduct of the war, the president, secretary of state, members of the Joint Chiefs of Staff, and MacArthur all were aware of the Chinese threats and to varying degrees dismissed them as bluffs. Though they have been eager to blame each other for the conduct of the

[37] Janis (1983, 58).

[38] The proximate cause of MacArthur's dismissal was a public disagreement with the administration over whether or not to accept a stalemate. However, the general had other disagreements with Truman, Acheson, and the Joint Chiefs. Early in August 1950, MacArthur engaged in an unauthorized trip to Taiwan, one which Christensen (1996, 179) documents was opposed by Truman, Acheson, and Bradley. Later that month, he sent a message to the Veterans of Foreign Wars on the strategic importance of Taiwan which Truman ordered him to withdraw. (See Acheson 1969, 422–4.)

[39] While political scientists continue to teach groupthink, and probably should, the evidence in the psychological literature is inconclusive. See 't Hart (1991) and Esser (1998).

war, none of these leaders has argued since that the others did believe the Chinese threats. The question thus remains: Why did so many U.S. leaders disbelieve the threats?

The evidence considered here suggests that China's diplomacy was an ineffective tool in part because it had a record of using it in a cavalier fashion. While U.S. assessments of China's intentions were affected by the military situation, U.S. leaders considered the possibility that the Chinese would intervene even with the existing balance of forces. The warnings from Foreign Minister Zhou, statements in the Chinese press, and movements of troops into Manchuria all failed to affect these assessments, however, in part because they resembled China's recent bluffs over Taiwan. As a result, China never was able to alter the original U.S. perception that its interests would not be served by intervening.

CONCLUSION

The Korean War ended with the signing of an armistice on July 27, 1952. De facto, the war resulted in a draw; the communists retained control of North Korea, but did not gain control of the south. The Chinese nevertheless attained a major goal: avoiding the long-term presence of U.S. troops on their border.

This chapter has argued that China's threats to enter the Korean War in the event that U.S. or UN troops crossed into North Korea were clear. U.S. leaders understood them, but nevertheless incorrectly dismissed them as bluffs. China's unfulfilled threats with regard to Taiwan were one reason for the lack of credibility of its threats to enter the Korean War; they encouraged some in the United States to see China's threats about Korea as just more bluffs. Moreover, if U.S. leaders had not dismissed China's threats, chances are good that China and the United States would have avoided a costly extension of the Korean War.

In the face of China's threats, the Truman administration's problem was to discern whether or not China's leaders truly were prepared to fight over North Korean independence. This task was made more difficult by the fact that China had an incentive to threaten to enter the Korean War, whether or not it really intended to do so. In retrospect, it is clear that China's threats were honest statements of its intentions. However, if China had not intended to enter the war in the event that U.S. troops crossed the parallel, it might nevertheless have succeeded in keeping those troops out of North Korea by bluffing. Whether honest or not, China's threats, if credible, might well have accomplished its goals at very little cost.

Though a case of failed diplomacy, China's attempt to deter U.S. forces from crossing the parallel helps to shed light on why diplomacy often succeeds. When states disbelieve each other's threats, they do so because adversaries in a crisis have incentives to bluff. If an adversary is likely to be bluffing, then it is reasonable to discount that adversary's threats. However, states also have strong incentives to tell the truth, even in the context of an international dispute. Like China prior to the Korean War, a state that threatens and does not follow through can acquire a reputation for using its diplomacy dishonestly. A state that bluffs thus jeopardizes something extremely valuable: the ability to threaten and to be believed. Without its recent history of unfulfilled threats over Taiwan, China might have accomplished its goal—keeping U.S. forces below the parallel—without fighting an unwanted war with the United States.

As the next chapter explains, a state often will tell the truth to avoid the risk of acquiring a reputation for bluffing. Because states often tell the truth, other states can expect that most diplomacy is honest—and can believe most of the threats they hear. When a state does acquire a reputation for bluffing, however, its adversaries are less likely to believe its diplomacy in the near future. Under this circumstance, a tragedy like the extension of the Korean War that occurred in the fall of 1950 is more likely.

CHAPTER 3

A Reputational Theory of Diplomacy

As THE PREVIOUS CHAPTER illustrated, states that recently have been caught bluffing have difficulty convincing others that this time is different than the previous one, that they consider the present issues more important and their present threats are not bluffs. Paradoxically, the existence of reputations for bluffing allows diplomacy sometimes to be credible; the desire to avoid a reputation for bluffing leads states to use diplomacy in a straightforward manner much of the time.

This chapter presents a reputational theory of diplomacy. I show that diplomacy is effective precisely because it is so valuable. When states are irresolute, they are tempted to bluff, but the prospect of acquiring a reputation for bluffing often keeps a state from doing so. A state that has a reputation for bluffing is less able to communicate and less likely to attain its goals. To maintain their ability to use diplomacy in future disputes, state leaders often speak honestly.[1]

States sometimes do bluff, of course. It is impossible to measure how often they do so because opponents and researchers may not discover when a successful deterrent threat was a successful bluff. The theory that I present here shows that diplomacy, whether it be honest or a bluff, is most likely to succeed when a state is most likely to be honest. A state is most likely to be honest when it has an honest reputation to lose, a reputation gained either by having used diplomacy consistently in recent disputes, or by having bluffed successfully.

Since a state that uses diplomacy honestly cannot be caught in a bluff, concessions to an adversary can be a wise policy. When a state considers an issue relatively unimportant and the truth is that it is not prepared to fight, bluffing carries with it the possibility of success but the risk of decreased credibility in future disputes. The term "appeasement" has acquired a bad name, but not all states in all situations are even deterrable. Many scholars believe that Hitler would have continued his onslaught regardless of Britain's actions in response to Hitler's activities in Czechoslovakia.[2] If the British had tried to bluff over Czechoslovakia, their attempts to deter an attack on Poland would have been even less credible.

---

[1] See Jervis (1970, 80).
[2] Rich (1973).

Because states are engaged in a continuing series of international inter-actions, and because they care different amounts about different issues, they are able to use diplomacy to obtain a beneficial trade of issues over time. States' leaders tend to say so when they consider issues unimportant (to acquiesce), and this allows them to indicate credibly when they con-sider issues to be crucial. Thus, each state tends to attain its goals more often when it considers itself to have greater interests at stake.

This chapter studies diplomacy using a game-theoretic model of inter-national interactions. I use the model to investigate why and when states can change each others' minds about valuable information in international disputes using verbal threats to use force. Unlike most other mathemati-cal models of crisis behavior, this one examines states that are engaged in a series of disputes over time, potentially with different adversaries. The repeated game has an important advantage: in a repeated game, states' past behavior and concerns about future repercussions can influence their present behavior and that of other states. Thus, for example, reputations are endogenous to my model, whereas in models of isolated disputes they are merely assumed.[3] In contrast to these others, my model implies that states' behavior is entirely different when a state has been caught bluffing in a recent dispute. For example, when a state recently has been caught bluffing, its deterrence is less likely to succeed.

REPUTATIONS FOR HONESTY AND REPUTATIONS FOR RESOLVE

I have explained that states usually begin international disputes unsure about each other's resolve, or willingness to fight, over the particular issues that are at stake in the dispute at hand. One important purpose of diplomacy is to communicate to an adversary a state's resolve to fight in the present situation. In this chapter, I show why states often are honest about their resolve, and thus why they are able to learn from each other's diplomacy. Reputations for honesty play a key role in my explanation: states often use their diplomacy honestly in order to avoid losing these reputations, or acquiring reputations for bluffing that would harm their

[3] For an example of a work that assumes the existence of a reputation by considering a single dispute in isolation, see Fearon (1992). For political-science works that model rep-utations for resolve using multistage games, see Nalebuff (1991); Powell (1990); Morrow (1989); and Alt, Calvert, and Humes (1998). Huth (1988) and Leng (1993) also devote attention to the form in which past behavior affects the present. A large literature in eco-nomics also examines the formation of reputations; unlike in my model, reputation in these models usually is tied to, but not perfectly correlated with, some enduring quality of the rep-utation holder. For an excellent review as of the mid-1980s, see Wilson (1985). Following Axelrod (1984), regime theory has relied extensively on insights from the infinitely repeated Prisoner's Dilemma.

ability to use diplomacy in the future. I also show that a state is better able to use diplomacy to communicate its resolve when it enters a dispute with a reputation for honesty.

Deterrence theory also has been concerned with a kind of reputation, reputations for resolve. Reputations for honesty and reputations for resolve differ both in the ways in which they are acquired and in their effects. A reputation for honesty is an expectation, based on others' observation that the state recently has been honest (it has not been caught bluffing), that the state is likely to use diplomacy honestly in the present situation. In contrast, a reputation for resolve is a belief, based on others' observation that the state has acted resolutely, that the state is a resolute type of state; this translates into an expectation that the state will act resolutely in the present dispute and in future ones.

In this chapter, I concentrate upon the diplomacy of one group of states, those that are called "defenders" in international disputes. Remember from earlier that the challenger is the state that tries to change the status quo by issuing a demand coupled with a threat to use force if another state does not take the demanded action (e.g., give up a piece of territory). The defender is the state that the challenger threatens. The defender may or may not choose to counter-threaten that it will fight the challenger to prevent the challenger from obtaining its desired change; if the defender does so, its threat is called a "deterrent threat," or an attempt at deterrence.

A defender maintains its reputation for honesty if it uses diplomacy honestly or if it bluffs successfully; it acquires a reputation for bluffing only if it bluffs and is caught. Defenders are honest in two different ways. Under some circumstances, a defender is willing to acquiesce to an adversary's demand, to admit honestly that it is not willing to fight over a disputed issue. Under other circumstances, a defender honestly can claim to be quite resolute—that is, it threatens to defend a particular issue, and it follows through on its threat if the challenger attacks. When a state either admits that it is irresolute in the present crisis or follows through on its deterrent threat, other potential adversaries see it acting honestly and it maintains its reputation for honesty. When a state bluffs successfully in the present crisis, others do not learn that its alleged willingness to fight was a bluff, and it also maintains its reputation for honesty.

A state acquires a reputation for resolve primarily by fighting. Though deterrence theorists differ on what constitutes resolve, or a willingness to fight, several maintain that it is an enduring, dipositional quality, that some states generally are more willing to fight than others. States acquire reputations for resolve by fighting; the idea is that fighting demonstrates this enduring characteristic, since only resolute states are willing to fight.[4]

---

[4] See Schelling (1966) and the works cited in note 3.

For example, Schelling (1966, 56) argued that the United States would have to defend California from a Soviet attack in order to maintain its reputation for resolve; "there is no way to let California go to the Soviets and make them believe nevertheless that Oregon and Washington, Florida and Maine, and eventually Chevy Chase and Cambridge cannot be had under the same principle."[5]

The behavior that leads to a reputation for honesty thus differs from the behavior that leads to a reputation for resolve, though there is overlap. One key difference is that a state that acquiesces to a demand today acquires a reputation for being irresolute—that is, not willing to fight. In contrast, a state that acquiesces to a demand today acquires or enhances a reputation for honesty, because acquiescence is an honest indication that the state is unwilling to fight today. Similarly, a state that engages in no dispute today does not increase its reputation for resolve, since it has done nothing to prove its resolve. However, as I explain later in this chapter, a state that engages in no dispute today makes its reputation more honest; reputations for bluffing fade over time if the state is not caught bluffing again.

The effect of a reputation for honesty also differs substantially from the effect of a reputation for resolve. A reputation for honesty helps a state to use diplomacy successfully, and a reputation for resolve does not. When a state has a reputation for honesty, others expect that it is likely to use diplomacy honestly. Thus, others are more likely to believe its diplomacy, and it is better able to communicate its willingness to fight the present adversary over the particular issues that the states are disputing at present (in other words, to communicate its resolve to fight in the dispute at hand). That is, if a state begins a dispute believing that an adversary is irresolute, an adversary with a reputation for honesty is better able to communicate that it is more resolved to fight over these particular issues than the state had thought to be the case. A state is more likely to believe an adversary to be resolute at the start of a dispute if the adversary has a reputation for resolve. However, a reputation for resolve provides no advantage in communicating that it is more resolute than others had thought at the start of the dispute.

States need reputations for honesty because they often have information about their resolve that they would like to communicate to adversaries.[6] Because a state's view of the interests at stake is an important influence

---

[5] Underlying Schelling's argument is the assumption that resolve persists from crisis to crisis; some states possess more of it than others, and states can acquire reputations for being particularly resolute. Thus, by fighting over California, the United States would demonstrate its high level of resolve, and earn a reputation for resolve that would help it in future disputes.

[6] In fact, if leaders possessed all pertinent information, they would not engage in crisis bargaining and they would not go to war (Morrow 1989; Fearon 1995).

on its resolve, and because a state's interests vary considerably from dispute to dispute, a state's resolve differs substantially from one dispute to the next (Hopf 1994). If tomorrow's issue is more important to a state, then the state is likely to have greater willingness to fight in tomorrow's dispute. Even in the context of enduring rivalries, the issues at stake in a series of disputes never are identical; perhaps the international situation, or one state's domestic politics, has changed. When a state considers the interests at stake in a dispute particularly important, it would like to be able to communicate that information to the adversary in order to increase its chances of prevailing in that dispute.[7]

This book investigates only reputations for honesty; this chapter shows from a theoretical perspective that these reputations allow for effective diplomacy. It is possible, however, that states acquire both types of reputations. If so, the existence of reputations for resolve is unlikely to negate the importance of reputations for honesty. Later in the chapter, I discuss this issue from a technical standpoint. From a substantive standpoint, most situations are different enough that a state, for the most part, must learn anew whether or not its adversary is willing to fight in the present dispute; if an adversary knows the United States' resolve to fight over Iraq, it does not necessarily know the country's resolve to fight over Pakistan. States need reputations for honesty; reputations for resolve do not help them to communicate information about their resolve that is unknown to potential adversaries at the start of the present dispute. The empirical analyses that I present in the next chapter also support the idea that reputations for honesty influence the course of disputes in important ways.

In the game-theoretic model, I assume that states are trying to learn about each other's values for the disputed issues, one component of resolve. I further assume that each state's value for the issues is largely

---

[7] Nalebuff (1991) argues that the costs that states pay if they go to war are a key influence on their decision-making calculus. This argument essentially is one about resolve: the costs of fighting include lost lives of military personnel (and for some leaders, the related prospect of popular discontent) and the economic costs of sustaining a war effort. States differ in their anticipated costs of fighting for various reasons, including the strength of their militaries. The costs of fighting affect the course of an international dispute because they influence each state's resolve. All else equal, a state is more willing to fight, or more resolute, if it anticipates that it will pay only low costs if it goes to war. A reputation for having low costs would have a similar effect to a reputation for being resolute. That is, other states would expect a state with a reputation for fighting wars cheaply to be more willing to fight than a state without such a reputation. Moreover, in the real world, the costs of fighting vary considerably from dispute to dispute; for example, in the next dispute, it is often the case that the terrain is different, the domestic situation is different, and the adversary is different. Thus, the arguments that I make here about reputations for resolve apply to reputations about the costs of war as well.

unknown to the adversary and completely unrelated across disputes.[8] (A state's value for the issue in two disputes may be similar, but, if so, the adversary does not know ahead of time that they are similar.) These assumptions about resolve are useful for investigating reputations for honesty, though they would not be appropriate for investigating reputations for resolve. I make them for three reasons. First, my goal is to explain how states communicate the information that is unknown to the adversary at the beginning of a dispute. By assuming that a state begins the dispute knowing little about an adversary's value for the issues, I focus on how the unknown information is conveyed. Second, the assumption that resolve differs from dispute to dispute (it may or may not be the same; the adversary does not know) is more realistic for my model than the assumption that it is *identical* from dispute to dispute, an assumption that models of reputations for resolve usually make. The assumption that the state's resolve is identical in every time period is reasonable in models that represent multiple time periods within one ongoing dispute. However, in a model like mine, in which each time period represents a different potential dispute, the assumption that a state's resolve is identical from one time period to the next would be quite unrealistic; it would imply that the U.S. resolve to fight over California was identical to its resolve to fight over Vietnam.[9] Third, it is widely believed that states (or persons, or firms) can acquire reputations for having qualities that endure over time. By assuming that such persistent qualities do not exist, I show that there is a situational component to states' reputations—states can acquire reputations that are based on behavior that is not linked to an enduring quality.

If states do acquire both types of reputations, it seems likely that a state's reputation for resolve is relatively more important if it was acquired in a dispute with issues that are more similar to those in the current one.[10] This may explain the mixed results in empirical studies about reputations for resolve, many of which find that reputations matter only when accrued from prior behavior with the same adversary (Huth 1997). For this reason, the model I present here, which does not allow for reputations for

---

[8] In the model, the challenger knows the distribution from which the defender's value for the issues is drawn, and vice versa. A state's willingness to fight additionally depends upon several other factors, including the probability that it will win if the states go to war. The part of a state's resolve that is unknown to the adversary (and thus might be the subject of a reputation) is its value for the issues.

[9] A model of reputations for resolve (not honesty) in multiple international interactions could assume that resolve is related but not identical in some pairs of disputes and unrelated in other pairs. Such a model would be quite complicated (particularly if it allowed for an infinite number of possible international interactions over time); to my knowledge, none of the scholars who stress the importance of reputations for resolve has attempted to write it.

[10] This is because the idea of reputations for resolve relies on the assumption that a state's resolve is similar in multiple disputes.

resolve, is least likely to apply to cases in which states' issues are expected to be most similar. I include such cases in the empirical analyses in the following chapters because I believe reputations for honesty can affect most, if not all, cases. If reputations for honesty do not apply to these cases, their inclusion should add noise to the empirical analyses, prejudicing the results against my theory.

AUDIENCE COSTS, CHEAP TALK, AND DIPLOMACY

The recent literature on crisis bargaining has led to the impression, probably inadvertently, that signals must be costly to convey information and that verbal diplomacy is costly.[11] This literature, often referred to as the "audience-costs" literature, draws upon a literature in economics that shows the effectiveness of costly signals. Remember that a costly signal is one that directly (and negatively) affects the sender's payoff. For example, if a worker must spend $50,000 to acquire a college education, that education is a costly signal to employers that the worker is of high quality (Spence 1974).[12]

Some parts of the audience-cost literature give the impression that costly signaling is the only way that actors can reveal information. For example, Fearon (1994a, 579) argues, "In Spence's (1973) terms, mobilization (or any other move in a crisis) must be a *costly signal* if it is to warrant revising beliefs. Costless signals, which often include private diplomatic communications and sometimes more public measures, will be so much 'cheap talk' since a state with low resolve may have no disincentive to sending them."[13] Elsewhere he writes, "If the announcement itself has no effect on either side's payoffs [it is "cheap talk"], then it can be shown that in any equilibrium in which state A does not choose randomly among demands, A will make the same demand *regardless of what state B says*, and the ex ante risk of war will remain the same as in the game without communication by state B" (Fearon 1995, 396; italics added). While the intent of the audience-costs literature is to stress the importance of domestic politics, it

---

[11] This is true despite Smith (1998b), who explicitly models the impact of domestic audiences with costless signals.

[12] See Robert Gibbons's definition of costless signals below. A costly signal is one that is not costless.

[13] I would argue that most of the audience-cost models technically do not contain costly signals, and Fearon (1994, 590, footnote 2) seems to recognize this point. Nevertheless, his work has been widely interpreted as showing that signals must be costly to convey information, perhaps because of the statement I quote in the text. Thus, my argument that cheap-talk signals can convey information in crises is more novel than it should be (though see Kydd 1992; Smith 1998a; Morrow 1994, and Ramsay 2003).

seems to have led to a widespread perception in the field of international relations that signals must be costly to convey information.

Why are verbal threats sometimes credible? The audience-costs literature argues that the credibility of states' threats in international disputes stems from the presence of domestic "audiences"—in other words, publics who pay close attention to statements their leaders make about international issues and have the ability to remove the leaders from office if they are unhappy with those leaders' performance. These audiences, some works maintain, "punish" leaders for backing down from a threat; this punishment acts as a cost that makes diplomacy informative (Martin 1993; Fearon 1994a; Schultz 1998). (When leaders are punished, they suffer "audience costs.")

The present book establishes that costly signaling is not the only way states can reveal information. In reconceptualizing diplomacy as cheap talk, I suggest an alternative reason as to why states are able to use verbal (diplomatic) threats effectively: a state can acquire a reputation for using its threats honestly, and then leaders of other states are more likely to believe its threats in subsequent international disputes.

This reputational theory of diplomacy has different implications about which states are able to use diplomacy from at least some parts of the audience-cost literature. Because audience-cost theory relies on powerful and attentive domestic publics, some works in this literature suggest that threats made by leaders of democracies are more credible than those made by leaders of autocracies (Fearon 1994a). The reasoning is that the latter cannot be voted out of office, and so do not suffer such severe audience costs. Because my theory stresses the importance of international rather than domestic audiences, it explains why both democracies and autocracies can use deterrent threats credibly and successfully; there need be no difference between the two in their ability to convey their intentions in the course of an international dispute.

My theory raises questions about a key assumption that is made by several works on audience costs, the assumption that audiences punish leaders who back down from threats. As I show here, diplomacy often works because states acquire reputations for bluffing, and states try to avoid such reputations. Nevertheless, bluffing sometimes is a state's best policy. When, on balance, backing down is best for a state, most leaders and domestic audiences should support it. However, when war is best for the state, most members of both categories should favor it. In neither case do domestic audiences as a group have a reason to punish leaders.

Smith (1998b) provides one possible foundation for the idea of audience costs; he argues that domestic audiences punish leaders who back down because leaders' willingness to threaten and to fight is a signal of their foreign-policy competence; competent leaders expect to do well if the states go to war and so press on, while incompetent leaders expect to fare poorly and so back down.[14] According to this argument, leaders have a disincentive to back down from their threats; doing so makes them look incompetent. My formal analyses do not challenge the logic of this argument; instead, my explanation of credible diplomacy is an alternative to the one that it provides.[15]

The remainder of this book demonstrates the role of international audiences—states—in establishing credibility. I do not show that costly signals or domestic audiences are unimportant—merely that international audiences matter. In fact, I believe that both international and domestic audiences influence leaders' actions.

Before turning to the model, a discussion of the effectiveness of cheap talk in conveying information is warranted. The point that cheap talk can be effective is not new; a literature in economics has examined the effectiveness of cheap-talk (costless) signals.[16] As Robert Gibbons writes:

> The key feature of such a cheap-talk game is that the message has no *direct* effect on either the Sender's or the Receiver's payoff. The only way the message can matter is through its informative content: by changing the Receiver's belief about the Sender's type, a message can change a Receiver's action, and thus indirectly change both players' payoffs.[17]

Diplomacy fits this definition well. A leader's phone call does not directly affect his or her state's well-being. Rather, it works because it often has repercussions. If the phone call serves its purpose, it makes the state better off by changing the adversary's beliefs about the state's intentions and thereby changing the adversary's course of action. Of course, the phone call may have unwanted consequences; it may make the state worse off by changing the adversary's beliefs and actions in an undesired direction.

How does one state convince another? A defender's ability to convince a challenger stems from both its and the challenger's behavior and expectations of both itself and the challenger. A challenger will believe a defender's threats only if the challenger expects the other to be using diplomacy honestly. Some honesty is a prerequisite for effective diplomacy. For diplomatic threats to make a difference, states that threaten must be more likely to fight than those that do not.

---

[14] Of course, one also might argue that competent leaders expect to do better in peace.

[15] See Guisinger and Smith (2002) for a model that combines the reputational theory that this book presents with a model of domestic politics.

[16] Crawford and Sobel (1982); Farrell and Gibbons (1989). For examples of cheap-talk models in political science, see Austen-Smith (1990, 1992). The model in this chapter differs from standard cheap-talk games but was motivated by that literature's idea of common interests.

[17] Gibbons (1992, 212; italics in original). Gibbons is a co-author of one of the seminal articles on cheap talk; see Farrell and Gibbons (1989).

The cheap-talk literature shows that communication through words and other costless signals is more likely when the speaker and the listener have interests in common. If two parties have the same goals, the speaker has an incentive to speak honestly and the listener has no reason to doubt the speaker's information. For example, during the Persian Gulf War, the United States agreed to provide Israel with early warning of Iraqi missile launches against Israel.[18] The United States had an incentive to give truthful information because it wanted the Israelis to be able to defend themselves. Israel, in turn, had every reason to trust the information.

When the listener may use the information to the speaker's disadvantage, the speaker has an incentive to lie. Incentives to lie are stronger when states have more divergent preferences. Again in the Gulf War, the Iraqis dramatically announced that coalition forces had hit a "baby milk" factory. The United States countered that it had hit only the part of the factory producing biological weapons. In this case, it is possible that each party was less than fully honest in an effort to manipulate the United States' partners in the coalition.[19]

In an international dispute, interests are neither perfectly aligned nor perfectly incompatible. Each state prefers to have the issue decided entirely in its favor. However, because war is costly, there is always some resolution, or bargain, that each would prefer to fighting if it had full knowledge of the situation (Fearon 1995). Moreover, each state engages in a number of disputes over time with different adversaries, though not all of these disputes become crises or wars. Over time, the possible "bargains" are greater in number and more complicated; it is possible for one state to lose territory today but be compensated by gains from a different adversary in the future.

As the cheap-talk literature shows, interests do not have to be perfectly aligned for communication to occur. Actors in a situation with mixed interests have incentives to misrepresent their preferences, but they also have incentives to tell the truth, and the latter are strong enough that others can learn from their words.

THE GAME-THEORETIC MODEL

The model rests on five main assumptions:

1. *War is costly.* The costs include lives lost and weaponry and other resources used.

---

[18] Freedman and Karsh (1994).
[19] Ibid., 319.

2. *Leaders care more about some issues than about others.* States engage in disputes about different issues across time, and these are of varying importance. For example, leaders usually consider home territory more important than other territory; Vietnam was more important to the North Vietnamese than to the United States. As Schelling has argued, it usually is easier to establish credible deterrence than credible extended deterrence for this reason.[20] A state also may consider one ally more important than another. Sometimes, security issues may be most important; at other times, domestic politics may make symbolic or ideological issues primary.

3. *Leaders are unsure of the value that other states place upon the issues.* In particular, at the start of a dispute, states do not know each other's value for the disputed issue precisely enough to know whether or not the adversary is prepared to fight. A state cannot precisely infer an adversary's value for the issue from information gathered in previous disputes; even if the issues under contention in two disputes are similar, they are never the same. For example, the disputes in Europe over the Balkans prior to and at the start of World War I differed in a variety of ways.[21] Thus, in each dispute, an adversary must attempt to ascertain anew whether or not the state values the issue highly enough that it is prepared to fight.

4. *States believe that positive probability exists that they will still be engaging in international relations tomorrow.* Tomorrow's interaction need not be with the same allies or adversaries as today's.

5. *Each state interacts with many others over time, and tomorrow's interaction is unlikely to be with the same state as today's.*[22] The assumption does not imply that *each* state interacts with every other, only that each state interacts with many others over time. The states in the model could represent any state, or, for example, the states in a particular region.

This last assumption simplifies the analysis but it is not necessary for the results. Without the assumption, the challenger and the defender in the model would represent the same two states engaging in disputes about different issues across time. In that case, the argument and the equilibrium proofs still hold. The model would then explain how reputations arise between two states and lead to effective diplomacy.[23]

---

[20] Schelling (1966, 33).

[21] See Albertini (1952, 577); Turner (1970, 95).

[22] In technical language, the assumption is that the opportunity for disputes arises "purely randomly" between any pair of states in two interacting groups.

[23] The literature on reputations for resolve questions whether or not reputations generalize (Huth, 1997). Do states pay attention only to interactions that involve particular adversaries or regions, or do they take note of all interactions? For the reasons I have discussed, the model here shows that any of these kinds of reputation is logically possible.

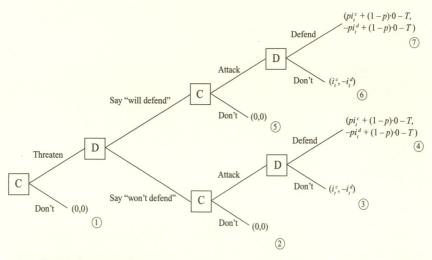

Payoffs: (Challenger's, Defender's)

C: Challenger's decision node
D: Defender's decision node

Parameters:
p: Probability with which the challenger is expected to win if war occurs
T: Cost of fighting, which both states pay in case of war
i_t^c, i_t^d: Challenger's and defender's values for the territory or other issues in this iteration, respectively. Note that the defender loses its value for the issue if it gives up through acquiescence, war, or backing down. In case of war, its expected value is $-pi_t^d - T$.

FIGURE 3.1. The Stage Game

The model describes a series of international interactions between states. In each interaction, both the use of diplomacy and the use of force are possible. The "stage game," depicted in figure 3.1, represents a one-period interaction between a randomly chosen "challenger" and a randomly chosen "defender." Many deterrence models, purely verbal and formal, share a similar form.[24] The repeated game consists of an infinite number of repetitions of the stage game—that is, in each period, each state believes that there is a positive probability that it will interact with some other state tomorrow.[25]

At the beginning of each new interaction (period, or iteration of the stage game), a challenger meets a defender. This meeting represents a situation in which two states happen to interact at a given time. Each

[24] For example, see Russett (1963); Schelling (1966); Huth (1988); Bueno de Mesquita and Lalman (1992); Morrow (1989).
[25] Formally, the discount factor, δ, is strictly positive.

challenger is drawn from a pool of potential challengers and each defender is drawn from a pool of potential defenders. At the start of the interaction, the defender possesses the territory or otherwise is satisfied with the status quo on the disputed issue. Each interaction may or may not become a dispute, then a crisis, then a war. At the beginning of the interaction, each state knows the other's relevant history; it knows of any speeches made and of all actions in its opponent's previous two interactions.

At the beginning of a new interaction, each player also "receives" a new value for issue at stake. This represents the extent to which the state values the issue that is the subject of the interaction. Each knows how important it considers this issue but it does not know its adversary's value for the issue; it knows only that its opponent has a value equally likely to be anywhere between zero and one. The challenger's issue value in this time period is i_t^c and the defender's is i_t^d.[26] A state's valuation of an issue is called its "type."

Each state plays in each period, though its potential adversary and its value for the issues are newly drawn from the relevant pools. That is, each country has some international interaction in each period, but tomorrow's interaction is likely to be with a different state over different issues.

Each interaction begins with a "talk" stage. In the stage game in figure 3.1, the challenger moves first, deciding whether or not to turn the interaction into a crisis, or militarized dispute. The interaction becomes a dispute if the challenger makes a speech threatening to attack if the defender does not resolve some issues in the challenger's favor. If the challenger does not threaten, the game ends with the status quo maintained, and each state receives a one-period payoff of zero. The challenger receives a payoff higher than zero if the states change the status quo, while the defender receives one lower than zero.[27] If the challenger does threaten, the defender responds with its own speech; it says either that it "will defend" or that it "won't defend" if an attack occurs. If the defender says, "won't defend," it acquiesces to the challenger's demands and gives up the issue.

The challenger then may attack. If it does not do so, the status quo is maintained, and each player has a payoff of zero for this interaction (time period). If the challenger attacks and the defender resists, war occurs. The challenger has a predetermined probability of winning (p); the probability

---

[26] More formally, at the beginning of time t, the challenger learns its value for the issue i_t^c and the defender learns its value i_t^d, where i_t^c, $i_t^d \sim unif[0, 1]$. Each state's value is private information. The upper and lower bounds are chosen for sake of mathematical convenience since the payoffs are Von Neumann-Morgenstern utilities and hence unique only up to a positive affine transformation. Two points on the scale can be chosen arbitrarily.

[27] Technically, a state can receive a payoff of zero from a change in the status quo if its value for the issue is exactly zero. This happens with probability zero in the model.

of winning is a function of the balance of forces between the two states.[28] If the challenger wins, it acquires the issue (adding i_t^c to its payoff) and the defender loses it (subtracting i_t^d). If the defender wins, which occurs with probability $(1 - p)$, then the status quo is maintained and both players receive a payoff of zero. No matter which wins, both pay the costs of war (subtracting T from their payoffs). Thus, the challenger's one-period expected payoff from war is $(p * i_t^c + (1 - p) * 0 - T)$ and the defender's one-period expected payoff is $(p * (-i_t^d) + (1 - p) * 0 - T)$. If the defender backs down, the issue is resolved in the challenger's favor without war. The challenger gets a one-period expected payoff of i_t^c and the defender gets a one-period payoff of $-i_t^d$. (For simplicity, the model assumes that an attack with no defense amounts to the defender giving up the issue.)

As in Gibbons' definition of a cheap-talk game, a defender's message in this game has no direct effect on payoffs. The states have the same subsequent choices of action whether or not the defender tries to deter an attack. The defender's payoffs are the same if the challenger attacks, regardless of whether or not the defender has tried deterrence. Similarly, the defender's payoffs are the same if the challenger does not attack, regardless of whether or not it has tried deterrence. Any difference in expected payoff comes not directly from the defender's message, but from the fact that the message influences the challenger's beliefs about the defender and thus the challenger's subsequent behavior.

When this interaction is over, each state begins another. Remember that the state's type does not persist from one dispute to the next. At the beginning of time $(t + 1)$, the state will interact with a new potential adversary and the issue at stake will be different. Neither state in any interaction exactly anticipates its last time period in the international system; it does not know when it will cease to exist and thus to interact with other states. From a technical perspective, this means that the game is infinitely repeated. I assume a common discount factor, δ.

EFFECTIVE, CHEAP DIPLOMACY

Even states involved in disputes have common interests over time. While each state prefers to have all issues go its way, in practice such one-sidedness is usually impossible. Each state has a particular interest in obtaining a favorable resolution of those disputes in which it considers the issues the most important. Since the outcome of war is uncertain,

---

[28] The assumption that p is fixed is made for analytic tractability. A modified version of the game that relaxes the assumption of fixed p is available from the author. The results discussed in this book carry over to the modified game.

a state is better off if it achieves deterrence success more frequently when it considers the issues more important. A state that considers an issue crucial sometimes finds itself interacting with one that cares much less. But the second state someday will find itself in a similar situation: considering an issue extremely important and facing an opponent that does not. All states can be better off over time if they are more likely to concede when issues are relatively unimportant to them and to get their way on issues they consider relatively important. This process is a type of "trade" of issues over time.

States' communications often are effective because of an entrenched pattern of behavior. States assign to others reputations for bluffing or for honesty based on the behavior that they observe others engaging in. States disregard the pronouncements made by other states that have bluffed recently and been caught. Since they have no "honest" reputation to lose, states that recently have been caught bluffing are more likely to bluff again. Thus, it is rational for listeners to be suspicious of their threats.

Since states benefit from diplomacy when it works, the possibility of acquiring a reputation for bluffing provides an incentive for states to use diplomacy honestly. When states do not have reputations for bluffing, they tend to use diplomacy honestly. Thus, when a state without a reputation for bluffing (with a reputation for honesty) maintains that it considers the issue at stake to be worth a fight, its adversary knows that this statement is likely to be true. It is in the listener's interest to heed the warning; otherwise, the listener is likely to end up at war.

Of course states do bluff—even states with reputations for honesty. However, states with reputations for honesty bluff rarely enough that others can learn from their threats. I elaborate this logic below using the formal model.

Equilibrium Selection

Finding a logical outcome of this situation amounts to finding an equilibrium of the model. As with all infinitely repeated games, this one has many equilibria. Scholars disagree about which equilibrium will be played when a game has multiple equilibria.[29] My approach is to choose

---

[29] There is widespread agreement that some equilibria will not be played—for example, equilibria that involve players making choices off the equilibrium path that they would refuse to make if they had the chance.

One possible criterion for equilibrium choice is Pareto optimality. One might speculate that every communicative equilibrium of this game also is Pareto superior to the equilibria in which no communication occurs (babbling equilibria). This is not the case; because only the defender communicates in the equilibrium I examine, the challenger actually is worse off with communication than without it. However, Sartori (2001) shows the existence of a

an equilibrium for substantive reasons and to use empirical analyses to determine if the patterns of behavior associated with this particular equilibrium are found in the real world. That is, I see the equilibrium and the model combined as an explanation which must be subjected to empirical tests.

As is common in political science, this approach is partly inductive and partly deductive. From general knowledge about the world, I speculated that a pattern of behavior something like that described in the equilibrium might exist. I created a model containing basic elements of the real world that I believe are essential to understanding states' behavior in international disputes and crises. Key among these are incomplete information about interests, and thus resolve; the fact that international interactions are not isolated events (states know that they will be engaged in international relations in the future); and the fact that such interactions involve different issues and potential adversaries over time. I then characterized an equilibrium of the model that corresponded roughly to the behavior that I initially speculated would exist.

Scholars often avoid infinitely repeated games because they have multiple equilibria. This can be a big mistake: there are some situations in which the repeated nature of interactions is key to understanding the behavior of political actors. The subject of this book is an example. One cannot understand the development of reputations without considering a series of interactions over time. One can, of course, assume that states foresee a last interaction, but this assumption is blatantly false in this situation and has substantial impact on the solution of a game.

While many (even infinitely many) equilibria can be equally reasonable from a technical standpoint, it is often the case that certain equilibria are particularly reasonable (or unreasonable) from a substantive standpoint. That is, inductive reasoning can lead the researcher to a choice of equilibrium. For example, any cheap-talk game has an equilibrium in which talk is meaningless, but it is substantively unlikely that states' threats never convey information.[30]

The formal analysis in this chapter does not show that the "theory"— the model and equilibrium combined—form a useful explanation of behavior. Rather, the formal analysis is the theory. The next chapter presents the results of empirical analyses that shed light on the usefulness of the theory.

---

similar communicative equilibrium with reputations for honesty in a modified Hawk-Dove game. Both the challenger and the defender can communicate in that equilibrium, and it is Pareto optimal.

[30] I discuss one equilibrium in which talk is meaningless in the appendix.

The Equilibrium

I characterize a perfect Bayesian equilibrium that corresponds to the substantive argument I made earlier in this chapter. PBE is a solution concept for games, like this one, in which some players have information that others lack. In a PBE, players update their beliefs rationally, according to Bayes's rule, whenever Bayes's rule applies. Their actions must be rational at each point in the game, given their beliefs.[31] I use the technique of factorization, which allows one to characterize equilibria of infinitely repeated games.[32] Technical analyses are presented in the appendix.[33]

To show formally that cheap-talk diplomacy can be effective, I characterize an equilibrium in which the defender's threats often convey information to the challenger about the defender's value for the issue at stake. In the equilibrium that I study, states play differently after two different histories. When the defender recently has not been caught bluffing (any outcome except 6 in figure 3.1), it has a reputation for honesty. It and the challenger engage in one pattern of behavior. Under this circumstance, if the defender counter-threatens the use of force, the defender's threat convinces the challenger that it is more resolved (more likely to fight) than it had previously believed to be the case. When the defender recently has been caught bluffing (outcome 6 in figure 3.1), it has a reputation for bluffing. It and the challenger engage in a second pattern of behavior, and its threat, if any, does not convey any information to the challenger.[34]

I define two concepts. A defender may bluff successfully or it may be caught. In the game, a defender *bluffs* if it says that it "will defend" without intending to follow through if the challenger attacks. A defender

---

[31] More technically, the players' strategies must satisfy sequential rationality at every information set and their beliefs must be consistent with Bayes's rule at every information set to which it applies.

[32] Abreu, Pearce, and Stacchetti (1986, 1990). Abreu, Pearce, and Stacchetti discuss sequential equilibria, but their technique easily can be modified for the purposes of my game to characterize a perfect Bayesian equilibrium.

[33] The equations that characterize the equilibrium in this case are highly nonlinear. I solve numerically; the solution results in a set of equilibria, each one of which corresponds to a pair of values of the exogenous variables, {T, p}. The equilibria are all of the same form, described in the text and shown in figure 3.2; thus, to avoid confusion, I refer to them as "the equilibrium" in the discussion.

[34] Technically, these are history-dependent strategies. Partial communication occurs when the defender has not been caught bluffing recently and no communication occurs when it has been caught bluffing recently.

For reasons of tractability, I examine an equilibrium in which the challenger always threatens. The stage game effectively begins at the second node of the game tree as shown in figure 3.1. I ignore the possibility that the challenger, too, can communicate.

is *caught* bluffing in period *t* if: (1) the defender has begun the dispute with a reputation for honesty (the challenger is listening); (2) the defender says that it "will defend"; (3) the challenger attacks; and (4) the defender does not follow through. In figure 3.1, then, the defender is caught bluffing in period *t* if the outcome in that period is Outcome 6 and if the defender began that period with a reputation for honesty. In the equilibrium I examine, a reputation for bluffing lasts for two periods.

While the duration of the reputation for bluffing—two periods—is chosen for mathematical convenience, a reputation is relatively short-lived for substantive reasons.[35] On the one hand, for a reputation to exist, it must last for at least one period. On the other hand, it is implausible that the reputation would last forever; a reputation that lasted forever would correspond to a story in which a state caught bluffing *never* could use diplomacy again. In practice, a state does not lose its credibility for all time if it bluffs unsuccessfully once. For example, even after the Soviet Union backed down in the Cuban Missile Crisis, it did not abandon diplomacy thereafter. Thus, a plausible punishment lasts for at least one period but not forever.

In the part of the equilibrium in which the defender has a reputation for honesty, its diplomacy is partially effective. The defender often tells the truth, and so its diplomacy convinces the challenger that it is more likely to fight than the challenger had previously thought to be the case (though it does not convey to the challenger its precise value for the issue). Thus, the defender sometimes can succeed in deterring attacks, either honestly or by bluffing. However, a defender that bluffs may be caught—that is, the challenger may attack. By reducing the effectiveness of a state's diplomacy in the immediate future, a reputation for bluffing harms the state's ability to deter attacks, including its ability to bluff successfully. That is why a defender with a reputation for honesty bluffs only when the temptation to do so is very strong.[36] The challenger listens to the defender's diplomacy because it wants to know whether or not its adversary will fight. Since the defender often is honest in this situation, the challenger can learn something from the defender's threats.

In the part of the equilibrium in which the defender has a reputation for bluffing (the punishment phase of the equilibrium), its diplomacy is ineffective. In this situation, the defender cannot lose a reputation for

---

[35] Proofs of the central results about reputations and effective diplomacy do not depend on the length of the reputation; the results hold for any equilibrium of the form depicted in figure 3.2. The equations that characterize an equilibrium with a one-period reputation are available from the author; these have numerical solutions for many values of the exogenous variables.

[36] As I discuss later, the temptation to bluff is strongest when the defender cares a middling amount about the issues.

honesty because it has none. Thus, it has every incentive to bluff. Because of its desire to avoid being duped, the challenger does not pay attention to the defender's diplomacy. Under these circumstances, the defender bluffs more often and its threats (bluffs or truthful statements) are less credible.

Note that the "punishments" in this equilibrium are substantively sensible, unlike the common punishment schemes in infinitely repeated games. In my equilibrium, states "punish" those that are caught bluffing by refusing to listen; this makes sense because states that have been caught bluffing do not convey information through their words. (In technical terms, they are "babbling.") In many equilibria of infinitely repeated games, the states doing the punishing punish only in order to avoid being punished themselves. The states that must punish them, in turn, will do so only because they will be punished if they fail to punish, and so on.

The transition from the noncommunicative part of the equilibrium back to the communicative part represents the fading of a reputation for bluffing. As time passes, the defender regains its reputation for honesty and its incentive to use diplomacy honestly. Why should a reputation for bluffing fade? Empirically, one observes that they do. Theoretically, the fading of a reputation represents behavior that is optimal in the circular way that all equilibrium behavior is optimal. As long as the challenger believes that the defender will cease its bluffing behavior, it is in the challenger's interest to assign the defender a reputation for honesty; the challenger listens because it wants to know whether or not the defender will fight. As long as the challenger is willing to listen, it is in the defender's interest to use diplomacy honestly much of the time because the defender is more likely to attain its goals with communication. Thus, when the challenger is listening, the defender makes listening worth the challenger's time.

Figure 3.2 shows the equilibrium strategies more formally.[37] If the defender was not caught bluffing in time $(t-1)$ or $(t-2)$, both states play as shown in the top half of figure 3.2; if the defender was caught bluffing, both states play as shown in the bottom half of figure 3.2. Recall that the values of the possible issues are scaled to be between zero and one; the horizontal lines in figure 3.2 represent possible values of issues that could arise. A state whose issue value in the given dispute is in the specified range (e.g., between 0 and l) plays in the stage game as shown above that range. For example, if the defender can communicate, the challenger is

---

[37] Technically, a player's strategy in this game is a collection of thresholds, the stage-game strategies for player-types falling in each interval determined by the thresholds, and a rule for switching between good- and bad-reputation subgames. Without loss of generality, I assume that players with types precisely at the thresholds play the stage-game strategies of types immediately to their left in the figure.

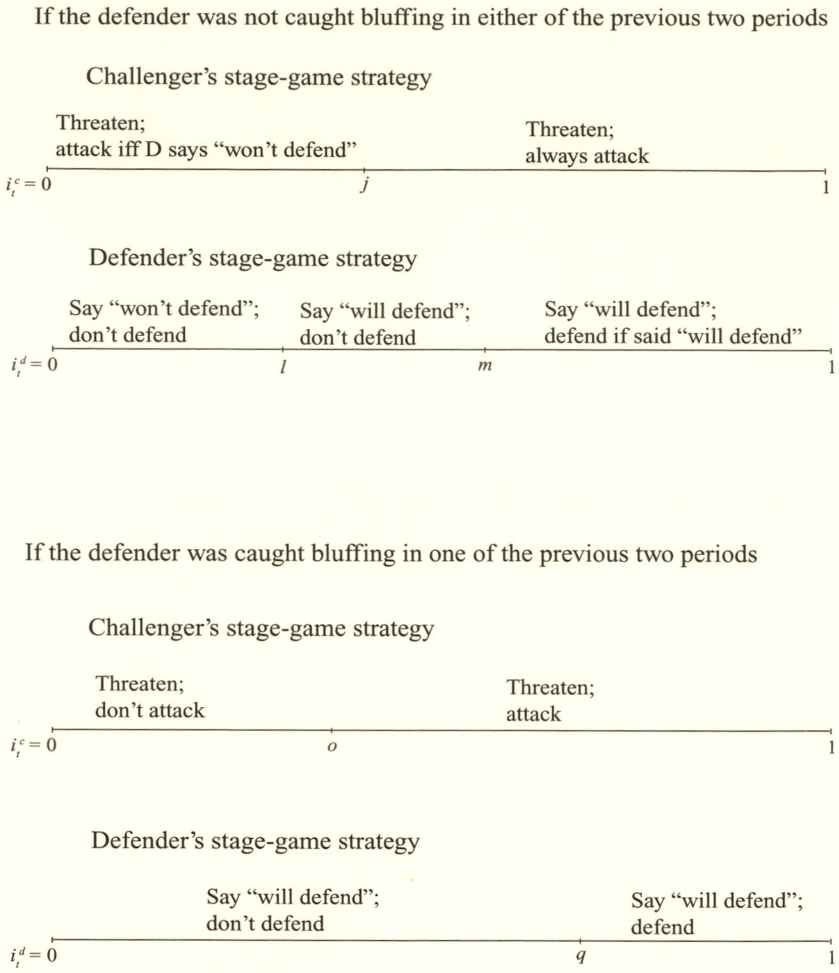

If the defender was not caught bluffing in either of the previous two periods

Challenger's stage-game strategy

Threaten;
attack iff D says "won't defend"

Threaten;
always attack

$i_t^c = 0$ j 1

Defender's stage-game strategy

Say "won't defend";
don't defend

Say "will defend";
don't defend

Say "will defend";
defend if said "will defend"

$i_t^d = 0$ l m 1

If the defender was caught bluffing in one of the previous two periods

Challenger's stage-game strategy

Threaten;
don't attack

Threaten;
attack

$i_t^c = 0$ o 1

Defender's stage-game strategy

Say "will defend";
don't defend

Say "will defend";
defend

$i_t^d = 0$ q 1

FIGURE 3.2. Equilibrium Strategies

deterred (challenges, but only attacks if the defender does not try deterrence) if it considers the issue at stake to be worth less than j.[38] Figure 3.2 presents the generic equilibrium, in which the thresholds are represented by letters (j, l, m, o, and q).[39] The precise thresholds depend upon the balance of forces (p) and the costs of war (T). For example, the defender always acquiesces when it considers the issue least important, but the

[38] Since the values for the issues are uniformly distributed, there is a j chance that a challenger is involved in a dispute over issues that are so unimportant to it.

[39] Sample equilibria are given in table A.1 in the appendix.

precise location of the cutoff l between issues that the defender concedes and issues over which it bluffs depends upon the balance of forces and the likely costs of war.

Efficacy of a Threat

The goal of a deterrent threat is to make a challenger less likely to attack than it was before hearing the threat. Loosely following Schelling,[40] I define the efficacy of a threat as the value-added of the defender's diplomacy. The efficacy of a deterrent threat is the *change* the defender's threat causes in the challenger's beliefs about the defender's likelihood of fighting. When the defender begins a dispute with a reputation for honesty (top of figure 3.2), the challenger begins a dispute believing that the probability that the defender will fight is $(1-m)$. By Bayes's rule, after hearing the defender say "will defend," it believes that this probability is $\frac{1-m}{1-l}$.

For the equilibrium shown in figure 3.2, the defender's threats have efficacy when the defender has a reputation for honesty. This fact is easily proven:[41]

1. Existence of an interior equilibrium implies that $0 < l, m < 1$.
2. $(1-m) < \frac{(1-m)}{(1-l)}$.

$\implies$ The defender's efficacy is positive.

The defender's threat serves to convince the challenger that the defender is more resolved than the challenger previously believed.

Similarly, the defender's threats do not have efficacy when the defender has a reputation for bluffing. The challenger begins a dispute believing that the probability that the defender will fight is $\frac{(1-q)}{(1-q)+(q-0)}$, or $(1-q)$. All defenders try deterrence, and $\frac{(1-q)}{(1-q)+(q-0)}$ of these do defend. The defender's efficacy is zero.[42] Thus, the game has an equilibrium in which reputations for honesty allow for effective, "cheap" diplomacy.

Effective diplomacy is not an inevitable outcome of international interactions. Though the communicative equilibrium that I study is a logical outcome of international interactions, the model has alternative equilibria in which states do not acquire reputations and diplomacy is completely ineffective. Thus, the model confirms the logic of an argument made by Hopf and others: since each dispute involves new issues, there is no logical reason why states' behavior today *must* be tied to how they behaved in

---

[40] Schelling (1960, 6).

[41] See the appendix for proof of existence of interior equilibria.

[42] The defender's efficacy is zero in any babbling equilibrium of this game since its threats convey no information.

the past.[43] Nevertheless, these kinds of equilibria are not equally plausible from an empirical standpoint, since states do obtain reputations for bluffing.

The model predicts that we will see bluffs and reputations for bluffing, but few of each. It also predicts that states will be more likely to bluff for a short time after they are caught bluffing (though they will not always do so); this is why they are less likely to obtain diplomatic success. While the next chapter tests the theory directly, these predictions seem to be in keeping with others' empirical observations. Axelrod and Zimmerman find little deception in the Soviet press about Soviet foreign policy over a thirty-five-year period.[44] Nevertheless, examples of bluffs do exist, often following other bluffs. For example, in 1962, India pursued a "forward policy," placing troops forward of Chinese outposts. China repeatedly threatened to respond with force and backed down. Accordingly, the Indian government dismissed Chinese threats as bluffs, even though China was the stronger power.[45] Indian General J. N. Chaudhuri said, "It was a game of Russian roulette, but the highest authorities of India seemed to feel that the one shot in the cylinder was a blank. Unfortunately for them and for the country it was not so. The cylinder was fully loaded."[46] The Chinese eventually attacked in what became the Sino-Indian War.[47]

States Do Bluff, but When?

The model clarifies the circumstances under which states are most likely to bluff. Of course, states that have reputations for bluffing are more likely to bluff than those that do not. However, even states with reputations for honesty sometimes bluff. They do so because bluffs sometimes succeed, and a state that succeeds in bluffing attains its goals at little or no cost.

Intuitively, many observers believe that states are most likely to bluff when they consider the issues at stake unimportant, but this intuition is incorrect. When a state has a good reputation to lose, it is most likely to bluff if it considers the issue moderately important—neither very unimportant nor crucial. This is so because a state with a reputation for honesty weighs the potential benefits of a successful bluff against the potential future costs of acquiring a reputation for bluffing. If it considers an issue unimportant, it is unwilling to risk a decreased ability to use diplomacy in the future to have the issue resolved in its favor. If it considers the issue

---

[43] Hopf (1994).

[44] Axelrod and Zimmerman (1981).

[45] Bueno de Mesquita and Lalman (1992, 200–202); Maxwell (1970, 226, 237).

[46] Maxwell (1970, 171).

[47] The model also explains the prevalence of acquiescence; Bueno de Mesquita and Lalman (1992, 68) find 109 cases of acquiescence among 707 international disputes.

extremely important, it truly is prepared to fight, and thus any threat to do so is not a bluff. If it considers the issue moderately important, however, it is neither willing to fight nor willing to acquiesce to maintain its reputation for honesty. In figure 3.2, a state with a reputation for honesty that has values for the issues between l and m bluffs; it is caught only $(1 - j)$ of the time, and it considers keeping an issue as important as l through m worth the risk.

Note that for a defender that bluffs—one that considers the issue to be between l and m in value—backing down from its threats is *always* the best policy if the challenger calls its bluff and attacks. This is precisely what it means to be bluffing; if the defender were prepared to fight, its threats would not be bluffs.[48]

Situational Reputations

Scholars usually argue that reputations are dispositional: they stem from underlying differences among people, firms, or states.[49] For example, Kreps and Wilson argue that monopolists may be strong or weak, and that they wish to develop reputations for strength in order to convince upstart firms not to enter the market.[50] Schelling suggests that states may be resolute or irresolute (and that resolve is at least partly an enduring characteristic), and that they wish to acquire reputations for resolve in order to increase their credibility in international conflict.[51]

In contrast, states in my model have no permanent differences in disposition. This difference reflects my belief that the crucial information in international disputes—how much the state values the disputed issue— varies substantially from one dispute to the next. Whether or not a state has the "will to fight" depends on what the issues are and so must be communicated anew through the use of diplomacy.

Since, by assumption, there are no enduring dispositions in my model, the reputations that emerge are situational. Defenders lie or tell the truth depending on the situation that they are in, and acquire reputations based

---

[48] My definition of a bluff differs from that of Bueno de Mesquita, Morrow, and Zorick (1997, 25), who argue that a state might learn something about its opponent that makes it change its mind, so that it was not bluffing, but "ex post the threat appears to have been empty." In my view, the defender's deterrent threat is usually a statement of a willingness to fight *even if the challenger is resolved*. If the defender is bluffing, its strategy is to say that it is willing to fight, but then to press on only against challenger whose behavior makes it look irresolute, backing down if the challenger's behavior makes it look resolute. Learning that the challenger is resolute does not change the defender's strategy; it merely changes the defender's observed actions.

[49] See Mercer (1996).

[50] Kreps and Wilson (1982).

[51] Schelling (1966).

on this behavior. Like a dispositional reputation, a situational reputation is an assessment based on past, observed behavior that a state is likely to behave in a certain way in the future. Situational reputations are no less rational than dispositional ones; since a defender that is caught bluffing actually is more likely to lie in the near future, it is rational to assign that defender a reputation for dishonesty.

Situational reputations could be considered a modeling simplification; they also may be an interesting real-world phenomenon. In their minds, leaders may attribute reputations for bluffing to disposition, thinking, "this state tends to lie." Such an error would be in keeping with my model; as long as leaders are less likely to believe the bluffer in its next interaction, the existence of reputations for bluffing in the international system will limit the amount of bluffing that occurs and make communication possible most of the time. Such an attribution error also would be consistent with portions of psychological theory that argue that persons over-attribute undesirable behavior to disposition.[52] A detailed comparison of the beliefs in this model with those in psychological theory is not explored here, and a precise match is unlikely to obtain. However, this consistency hints at similarities between rational-choice and psychological approaches to decision making.

Diplomacy, Commitment, and War

I suggested at the beginning of this chapter that diplomacy allows states to realize common interests. To pursue this line of reasoning, I now engage in a thought experiment: I compare the real world, in which states do communicate, to a hypothetical world in which communication is impossible. I do so by comparing two equilibria: the partially communicative equilibrium discussed earlier (which represents the real world), and an equilibrium in which states never can communicate (which represents the hypothetical world without communication). In the noncommunicative equilibrium, states play the strategies in the bottom half of figure 3.2 forever, rather than alternating between the two sets of strategies.

Two results related to states' well-being stem from the fact that credibility allows states to use diplomacy as a form of commitment. Commitment is a double-edged sword. The defender is less likely to suffer an attack when it can commit itself than when it cannot. However, for its diplomacy to be effective, it must be willing to follow through.[53] Thus, the

---

[52] On attribution error as a psychological bias, see Ross and Anderson (1982) and Fiske and Taylor (1984). For applications in political science, see Jervis (1976) and Mercer (1996).

[53] This argument is similar to an argument that Fearon makes about costly signaling: "audience costs and risks of preemptive war work to separate states according to resolve *precisely* by posing the risk of unwanted escalation" (Fearon 1992, 172).

defender gets more of what it wants when it can communicate. However, war can be more common with communication than without.[54]

For reasons of tractability, this chapter examines a situation in which the challenger cannot communicate. In an analogous equilibrium with bilateral communication, I conjecture that the logic of the equilibrium would carry over. The challenger, too, would obtain issues that it valued more over time, on average, with the help of communication. Thus, states would attain a "trade" of issues over time as suggested at the beginning of the chapter, conceding less-important issues and keeping or acquiring more-important ones.

The Model and the Real World: A Technical Discussion of Correlated Interests and Information

Like all models, this one is a simplification of reality rather than a complete description. This section discusses from a technical standpoint two simplifying assumptions that I make in the model: (a) that a state's value for the issues in one dispute tells potential adversaries nothing about its value in subsequent disputes; and (b) that the adversary knows little about a state's value for the issues at the beginning of the dispute.

As I noted earlier, it is likely that the interrelatedness of a state's resolve in two disputes varies with the disputes in question. The information that an adversary possesses about a state's resolve at the start of a dispute varies with the situation. These subjects are linked; to the extent that two disputes are interrelated, it is possible that a state can acquire a reputation for resolve that affects an adversary's beliefs about its resolve at the start of the second dispute.

One cannot know with certainty what the outcomes of a more complicated model would be without solving such a model; however, one can speculate. For theoretical reasons, I believe that my general argument still would hold if I were to relax these two assumptions. In other words, the general patterns of behavior found in the equilibrium I examine would occur in the more complicated model with these assumptions relaxed. I also believe that additional patterns of behavior would emerge, patterns that are not explained by my simpler model.

Though real-world behavior surely is more complicated than behavior in this model, the empirical results in chapter 4 also provide support for the arguments made in this chapter. If the patterns of behavior that I discuss did not occur in the more complicated real world, then one would not expect to see them occur in the empirical analyses. The next chapter shows that these patterns do occur; whether or not a defender recently has

---

[54] See the appendix for further discussion of these results.

been caught bluffing has a substantial impact on its credibility in future disputes.

CORRELATED INTERESTS

Assume for a minute that a defender's values for the issues at stake are correlated across disputes, but that this correlation is quite imperfect.[55] Since the country's interests are correlated, its resolve (willingness to fight) in one dispute is correlated with its resolve in the next. Since the correlation is imperfect, a state never can learn an adversary's present resolve completely by observing its past behavior. In a model with this assumption, there might be two "state" variables, by which the challenger would keep track of the state of the defender's reputation for resolve and its reputation for honesty.

In a model with reputations for resolve as well as for honesty, a defender would have additional incentives not to acquiesce to challengers' demands; acquiescence would decrease the value of its reputation for resolve. These additional reasons to stand firm pose a challenge to my theory: if the defender were to back down after stating an intention to fight, would the challenger assign it a reputation for bluffing? I conjecture that an equilibrium would exist in which the challenger did so. Due to the addition of reputations for resolve, the defender would be willing to acquiesce less often than in my model and equilibrium (and the cut-point for acquiescence, l, would be lower). Nevertheless, a reputation for honesty would remain valuable, since a defender's willingness to fight in a future dispute would not be revealed completely by the state of its reputation for resolve. In other words, some states that acquiesce in my analysis would fight to maintain their reputations for resolve, but others still would acquiesce, even at the cost to their reputations for resolve, in order to preserve the ability to communicate the unknown portion of their resolve in the next dispute. States' reputations for honesty probably would form in much the same way as they do in my model: a state would acquire or enhance a reputation for honesty by doing nothing, acquiescing, or following through on its threats. When the defender became involved in another dispute, the status of both reputations probably would affect its credibility, but in different ways. Looking at figure 1.1 on page 9, the status of a defender's reputation for resolve probably would affect the challenger's initial beliefs about the defender's willingness to fight. The status of a defender's reputation for honesty probably would affect the defender's ability to change the challenger's beliefs about its resolve using its deterrent threats.

---

[55] One also could allow the correlation to vary with the disputes in question.

If states do acquire reputations for resolve, there is no reaso assume that these reputations form or change in precisely the sam as reputations for honesty. For example, in discussions of reputations for resolve, Jervis questions the idea that backing down is bad for credibility, suggesting instead that states that have backed down will attempt to rebuild their reputations by fighting.[56] Since states that are rebuilding their reputations are more likely to fight, the diplomacy of states that retreated recently should be more rather than less credible. If states acquire reputations for resolve as well as reputations for honesty, it is possible that a state with a reputation for being irresolute might improve its reputation more quickly by acting resolved, leading to behavior similar to that described by Jervis.

As applied to the present work, however, Jervis's argument suffers from two main weaknesses. First, this behavior is not a logical outcome of my model. In my model, if states were to possess increased credibility after bluffing, then there would be no disincentive to bluff. Without a disincentive to bluff, states would bluff often and diplomacy never would be effective. More generally, in an equilibrium of this model, states' ability to regain their reputations for honesty cannot depend upon good behavior. Second, as the next chapter demonstrates, the historical record does not support the conjecture that states obtain a surge in credibility after bluffing. To the contrary, like China and Russia in the cases just discussed, states that have been caught bluffing obtain reputations for bluffing and suffer losses of credibility.

MORE INFORMATION AT THE START OF A DISPUTE

Now assume that a challenger begins a dispute knowing more about the defender's value for the issues at stake than it does in my model.[57] In my model, the challenger has beliefs that the defender's value for the issue is uniformly distributed between zero and one. Would the possession by the challenger of additional prior information lead my model or equilibrium to be inapplicable? In the equilibrium I examine, defenders concede some of the time and challengers learn from these concessions that the defenders are less resolved than previously thought to be the case. In a more-complicated model in which the challenger had more prior information about the defender's interests, would a defender's unwillingness to concede still provide information that the defender considered the issues

---

[56] For example, see Jervis (1997, 266–71).

[57] The questions of correlated issues and information are related. If a defender's interests in one dispute are known to be highly correlated with its interests in the next dispute that arises, then the challenger in the second dispute is more likely to begin that dispute with substantial information about the defender's willingness to fight.

more important—and was therefore more willing to fight—than the challenger previously had thought? Again, I conjecture that my equilibrium would hold for most cases.

First, consider a hypothetical dispute in which the challenger knows ex ante that the defender certainly considers the subject of the dispute so important that it is prepared to fight.[58] The purpose of the challenger's threat is to ascertain whether or not it can obtain a change in the status quo without going to war. If the challenger knows ex ante that the defender certainly is willing to defend, then it gains nothing from threatening the use of force; the challenger cannot convince the defender to give up the issues without a fight. If the challenger itself is prepared to go to war, it is likely to engage in a surprise attack, rather than to alert the enemy to its intentions. If the challenger is not prepared to go to war, it is likely to refrain from threatening the use of force, so that onlookers never see a crisis. These latter cases form a subset of the set of disputes that do not become crises, and my model does not explain them.

Now, consider a hypothetical dispute in which the challenger knows ex ante that the defender certainly considers the subject of the dispute so unimportant that it is unprepared to fight. Under this circumstance, the challenger might make a demand of the defender in order to indicate its desire to change the status quo on this issue. The challenger occasionally may couple this demand with a threat to use force, in an attempt to communicate its own willingness to fight. If so, one observes a crisis. Since the defender is unprepared to fight, it acquiesces to the challenger's demand. These cases form a subset of the set of crises in which the defender does not try deterrence, and my model also does not explain them.

In sum, if a challenger knows with certainty whether or not the defender is willing to fight in the present dispute, my theory does not apply. These cases are likely to consist of surprise attacks, and of subsets of those disputes in which a challenger never issues a threat (ones that do not become crises) and of crises in which the defender acquiesces to a challenger's demands.

As long as challengers begin disputes with some uncertainty about defenders' willingness to fight, which is the case in most disputes, they can learn from defenders' decisions to acquiesce or to issue deterrent threats. The fact that defenders tend to acquiesce when they care less about the

---

[58] One also can imagine alternative models in which each state begins a dispute uncertain enough about the adversary's value for the issues that it does not know whether or not the adversary is prepared to fight, but the prior distributions of values for the issues are not uniform. I consider the case of complete certainty here because it is this case that could potentially challenge the logic of my equilibrium. As long as there is uncertainty, the logic of the argument is straightforward, though solving a model with an alternative distribution is more complicated.

issues signifies that a defender that tries deterrence is more resolute than the challenger previously had thought to be the case.[59]

It is worth noting that ex ante and ex post uncertainty are not the same; my model applies as long as the states have uncertainty ex ante about each other's willingness to fight. For example, once one observes that a state has acquiesced, it is easy to be certain that it was willing to do so. However, the challenger usually did not have this information ex ante. Similarly, in many cases, one can see ex post that both the challenger and the defender were willing to fight. The challenger begins a dispute with uncertainty about the defender's interests, hoping that its initial threat will convince the defender to give up the disputed issues without a war. Though the defender tries to deter an attack, the challenger is not deterrable. It had hoped to acquire a change in the status quo through the cheaper method of diplomacy, but when deterrence fails, it goes to war. In this case, the outcome of the dispute is the same as if neither state had tried diplomacy: the states fight over the disputed issue. Nevertheless, neither state knew ex ante that the other state considered the issue important enough to be worth a fight, so that diplomacy was worth a try.

CONCLUSION

This chapter demonstrates the role that reputations for honesty play in crisis bargaining. I suggest that diplomacy works because it is beneficial, so that states have an incentive to preserve their ability to use it. Using diplomacy, states communicate information about which issues they consider particularly important and thus increase the chances of prevailing when these issues are at stake. The flip side of the coin is that states must concede those issues they consider less crucial; by doing so, they maintain credibility for disputes in which they consider the stakes higher.

This theory fills a gap in our understanding of crises by explaining why cheap-talk diplomacy can change an adversary's mind about a state's resolve. In doing so, it shows that diplomacy is a valuable tool by which states often attain their goals. States can use diplomacy to communicate information to adversaries about whether or not they are willing to fight. Their ability to communicate depends not only on the balance of forces,

[59] It is unclear whether or not states ever know with certainty whether or not their adversaries are prepared to fight. If they do occasionally have such knowledge, this poses no problem for the logic of my argument, though my model does not apply to any instances in which this is the case. In most disputes, the challenger is not completely certain about whether or not the defender is willing to fight. Since many defenders reveal new information when they state their willingness to acquiesce, others also reveal information whey they state their unwillingness to do so.

but also on whether or not they have recently been seen as using diplomacy honestly (whether or not they have been caught bluffing).

I do not argue that costly signals are meaningless, and the choice between cheap-talk and costly signals remains an important subject for future research. One conjecture is that a state will turn to costly signals when it has a reputation for bluffing and considers the issue exceptionally important—Russia at the beginning of World War I might be an example. Of course, if it were always possible to use costly signaling to avoid the repercussions of bluffing, then cheap talk never would be credible.

The model that I present in this chapter has novel, testable implications about states' behavior in international disputes. This chapter develops one central implication: a defender's attempt at deterrence is less likely to be effective and the defender is less likely to attain its goals when it has a reputation for bluffing. This reputations hypothesis differs from that of deterrence theory: my model suggests that acquiescing in one dispute leads to a reputation for honesty, and so is positively associated with success in the next dispute, while deterrence theory suggests that acquiescing in one dispute leads to a reputation for lacking resolve and is negatively associated with success in the next dispute. The reputations hypothesis also is contrary to audience-cost models, which suggest no association between a state's recent behavior and the outcome of the current dispute.[60]

The next chapter discusses the model's implications further and turns to testing the argument empirically.

[60] However, see Guisinger and Smith (2002).

PART III

Evidence That Honesty Matters

CHAPTER 4

Reputations for Honesty and the Success of Diplomacy

WHY CAN A STATE use diplomacy to change an adversary's mind about its willingness to fight now over the particular issues at stake? In the previous chapter, I argued that the ability to use diplomacy is a boon to states; when a state's diplomacy is effective, it attains its goals at little or no cost. States with reputations for honesty have incentives to use diplomacy honestly, in order to avoid acquiring reputations for bluffing, which would hurt their ability to use diplomacy in the near future. States' incentive to use diplomacy honestly when they have reputations for honesty explains *why* their diplomacy often is effective; potential adversaries expect these states to be honest, so they believe their threats.

Earlier in the book, I discussed the puzzling failure of China's attempt at deterrence during the Korean War. I noted that China's leaders stated quite openly and precisely that they intended to enter the war if U.S. forces crossed the 38th parallel into North Korea. Many U.S. leaders began the war believing that a fight over Korea was not in China's best interest.[1] The question, however, is why China's threats failed to change U.S. leaders' minds on this score.

The theory that I discussed in the previous chapter sheds some light on this question. China's difficulties in attaining deterrence were, in part, the result of China's unfulfilled threats over Taiwan prior to the Korean War. These unfulfilled threats hindered its ability to convince the United States that it intended to intervene in the Korean War. In general, states with reputations for bluffing are less likely to succeed in changing others' minds about their intentions. China's unfulfilled threats over Taiwan contributed to the widespread belief in the United States that China's threats to intervene in the Korean War were bluffs.

As I explained in the previous chapter, states with reputations for bluffing have a harder time with their diplomacy because they are, in fact, more likely to bluff. Yet, in the Korean War case, China clearly was not bluffing. Why did China honestly threaten to enter the war? China threatened because it hoped to deter the United States, and it entered the war because it had considerable interests at stake; it wanted to maintain a communist state on its Korean border. Though states with reputations for bluffing are

---

[1] See, for example, Rees (1964, 113).

more likely than other states to bluff again, states almost always follow through on their threats when they consider the disputed issues extremely important, regardless of their reputations.[2]

While chapter 2 argued that China had a reputation for bluffing, it noted that this reputation was by no means universal; many in the United States did believe that China intended to attack Taiwan. China's unfulfilled threats over Taiwan help to explain its lack of credibility in the Korean War, but they are only a partial explanation.

No political-science theory explains every aspect of any case, nor is one case enough to evaluate the usefulness of a theory that claims to explain states' behavior more generally. The present chapter turns to a larger set of international disputes and uses them to investigate the usefulness of the theory.

My theory explains why diplomacy works, but it also has implications about states' behavior over the course of international disputes. These implications are "testable"—that is, they can be evaluated using data. If my explanation of diplomacy is correct, then states should behave in international disputes in ways that the theory says they do. In particular, as I explained in the previous chapter, deterrence should be more likely to succeed when the defender has a reputation for honesty. Moreover, a defender should be more likely to follow through on its threats when it has a reputation for honesty.

I begin this chapter by discussing how these testable implications follow from the theory. I then describe the information and statistical technique that I use in this chapter to evaluate them. The data set contains information about international interactions between 1816 and 1993, including approximately 1,300 international disputes.

I next present statistical results to show that the world works in ways that the theory says it does:

- A typical defender with a reputation for honesty is more likely to deter an attack than a defender with a reputation for bluffing by roughly 21.5 percentage points.[3]

---

[2] Would China's threats over Korea have been more successful, had it not threatened Taiwan? Any answer to this question is speculative. Nevertheless, prior to these conflicts, U.S. leaders seem to have believed that China was more likely to fight over Taiwan than Korea. For example, Acheson lists the "lack of real advantage to China itself of coming in" as one of the reasons why he believed the Chinese would not enter the Korean War (U.S. Congress Senate 1951, 2000). If, in the early 1950s, China had said it was willing to let Taiwan live in peace, this news would have come as a surprise to the United States. If China soon thereafter had said that it was unwilling to tolerate U.S. troops in North Korea, U.S. leaders might well have concluded that preventing a U.S. occupation of North Korea was quite important to the Chinese.

[3] The reputations variable that I use can take on many values, as I explain later. By a

- A typical defender with a reputation for honesty is more likely to follow through on its threats than a defender with a reputation for bluffing by roughly 5.5 percentage points.

These results increase confidence in my theory of diplomacy; because it can explain broad patterns of states' behavior in international disputes, the theory is less likely to be wrong. Nevertheless, a skeptical reader might be concerned about the robustness or interpretation of these results. A final section of the chapter demonstrates that the results are robust along four main dimensions. First, the conclusions remain the same with the inclusion of several control variables that are suggested by other works on international crises. Second, they remain the same if I use either of two alternative definitions of a reputation for honesty. Third, the results cannot be due simply to differences among states in a propensity to be disputatious. Finally, my measure of a reputation for honesty does not simply capture the idea of a reputation for resolve.

CENTRAL EMPIRICAL IMPLICATIONS OF THE FORMAL MODEL

In the formal model, I conceptualize an international dispute in four steps: the challenger's decision about whether or not to threaten the use of force, the defender's decision about whether or not to counter-threaten (try deterrence), the challenger's decision about whether or not to attack after hearing the defender's threat, and the defender's decision about whether or not to defend if attacked. The equilibrium analysis focused on the defender's ability to communicate. Thus, the testable implications are about the states that are challenged and about their deterrent threats, rather than about the threat by the challenger that initiates the crisis.

In the equilibrium, a defender "babbles" when it has a reputation for bluffing; it uses diplomacy without care because it does not have a good reputation to lose. Having threatened, such a defender is more likely to back down. A defender with a reputation for honesty, on the other hand, tries to maintain that reputation; it is more likely to follow through on its threats. For example, when President Johnson told the Soviets in 1968 that the United States was committed to the defense of Berlin, though not of Czechoslovakia, Johnson's statement was meaningful; the United States was likely to fight if the Soviets attacked Berlin (National Security Council 1968). This logic leads to the following implication:[4]

---

defender with a reputation for bluffing, I mean here a defender that has more of a reputation for bluffing than 90 percent of other defenders.

[4] I discuss these implications more formally in the appendix.

Implication 1. A defender with a reputation for honesty is more likely to defend following a deterrence failure than is a defender with a reputation for bluffing.

I define reputations as in the game-theoretic model of chapter 3:

> A defender acquires or increases a reputation for bluffing if it threatens and backs down when a challenger attacks. It maintains a reputation for honesty if it acquiesces to the challenger's demands; if it threatens, the challenger attacks, and it follows through on its threats to fight; or if it engages in a successful bluff (the challenger threatens to fight and it backs down).

A challenger considers the consequences of an attack, and a defender with a reputation for bluffing is a relatively good gamble. Because a defender with a reputation for bluffing is more likely to back down if deterrence fails, a challenger is more likely to attack such a defender. For example, China in the Korean War was a relatively good bet—having bluffed once, it was more likely to be bluffing again. (Tragically for the United States, this was not a bet that paid off.) Since, on average, defenders with reputations for honesty are more likely to follow through on their threats to fight, challengers are more likely to back down after hearing their threats. This logic leads to the following implication:

Implication 2. A challenger is more likely to attack following the defender's attempt at deterrence when the defender has a reputation for bluffing. (The defender's attempts at deterrence are more likely to fail when it has a reputation for bluffing.)

My theory also suggests that the balance of forces affects the progression of international disputes, but it does not provide a precise prediction about the form of the effect, as I discuss further in the next section. Thus, I simply test the hypotheses that the balance of forces affects each stage of dispute escalation.

Determining Empirical Implications of the Theoretical Model

The question of how to test formal models has attracted a lot of attention recently.[5] In the previous chapter, I explained that I consider the "theory" to be the combination of the game-theoretic model and the equilibrium that I characterize. I chose an equilibrium to characterize based on a behavior I believe exists in the world. Like most, if not all, models in political science, this approach is to some extent inductive; my broad idea

---

[5] For example, a recent National Science Foundation program funds research and two summer schools on this subject; a recent issue of *Political Analysis* was devoted to it (11:4, Autumn 2003).

for the equilibrium came from knowing something about the real world. Yet it is also deductive; the precise pattern of behaviors that emerges in the equilibrium was not in my mind before I characterized the equilibrium. My goal in this chapter is to test this theory, to evaluate the equilibrium choice, as well as the model, by comparing patterns of behavior that occur in the equilibrium to states' behavior in international disputes and crises.[6]

A key question in testing a theoretical model is that of which implications are "central" and should be tested empirically to determine the model's usefulness. A formal model like the game-theoretic model I described has numerous implications that can be tested empirically. Yet not all implications are equal when it comes to evaluating the model.

I choose implications as central based on their robustness to varying the model slightly and to varying the equilibrium slightly. Analogous to robustness checks in statistical models, the robustness checks I conduct to decide which implications to evaluate are based on my judgment of the most likely plausible similar equilibria and the most likely plausible alternative model.

While I consider the theory to be the equilibrium combined with the model, there are often some choices in characterizing an equilibrium that are arbitrary. In my case, the defender's precise form of "babbling" when it has a reputation for bluffing is such a choice. In my equilibrium, all defenders send the same message and so their threats are completely uninformative to the challenger. The defender's strategy could take many forms and still amount to babbling. Every type of defender could refrain from threatening the use of force; every type of defender could randomize, threatening the use of force with some probability p and refraining from doing so with probability $1 - p$; or every type of defender could threaten the use of force. In the equilibrium in the previous chapter, the defender always threatens the use of force when it starts a dispute with a reputation for bluffing. I chose this version of babbling because it is simple and because the version in which the defender never threatens seems unreasonable; one does not see defenders with reputations for bluffing refraining from ever issuing threats. However, if one substitutes any of the other types of babbling for this part of the defender's strategy, an equilibrium exists that is otherwise identical to the one I presented in the previous chapter.

The model combined with any of the "alternative" but extremely similar equilibria in which the defender threatens with positive probability when it babbles constitute essentially the same theory as the one given in

---

[6] When I discuss testing the "model" or "theory" in this chapter and the next, I refer to this combination of model and equilibrium.

the previous chapter. Thus, if an implication does not hold across these equilibria, I do not use it to test the theory.

Implications 1 and 2, presented earlier, are robust to this small change. Implication 2 relies on the fact that the defender babbles in equilibrium, that its threats are completely uninformative, but not on the specific form of the babbling. However, because it is not robust to this change, I rule out another implication as a criterion for evaluating the theory: the implication that the defender always threatens the use of force when it has a reputation for bluffing.

I also consider robustness to using an alternative model that relaxes the assumption that I consider substantively the most problematic. This assumption involves the balance of forces (p in the model). In the formal model that I use to study diplomacy, each iteration represents a new dispute, but the probability that the challenger wins (the defender loses) if war occurs is fixed from iteration to iteration. Because I am interested in how the outcomes of one dispute affect what happens to the defender subsequently, the assumption that the balance of forces is fixed across the defender's disputes could be misleading. For example, the defender may be a minor power that is involved in a dispute today with a slightly more-powerful challenger. If so, the balance of forces favors the challenger, but the defender might seize the opportunity to fight a war against this challenger because the defender expects a less-favorable balance of forces in future disputes.

As a robustness check, I modify the basic game slightly so that the balance of forces today may differ from the balance that the defender expects to face if it becomes involved in future disputes.[7] An equilibrium of this modified model exists that is almost identical to the one I characterize in the previous chapter. In it, states play the strategies as depicted in figure 3.2. Implications 1 and 2 are robust to this slight change in models. However, the model and equilibrium of the previous chapter have other implications that I do not use to evaluate it because the implications are not robust to this change. These implications concern the impact of the balance of forces and the costs of war on the challenger's decision to attack

---

[7] I modify the game by introducing a parameter p', the probability that today's challenger wins a war against today's defender if such a war occurs. In this modified version, p represents the defender's probability of losing a war, should war occur, in any future dispute. In other words, today's balance of forces (p') may differ from the balance that the defender expects to face if it becomes involved in future disputes (p). The modified model captures the fact that the balance of forces between the defender and the current challenger may represent an unusual opportunity or an unusual problem for the defender in question. However, today's dispute also may be "average" (i.e., p can equal p').

The modified game is available from the author upon request. The model presented in the previous chapter is simpler and a more straightforward exposition of my central points.

(the probability of deterrence failure) and on the defender's decision to defend if deterrence fails. These factors affect the states' decisions in both versions of the model, but the predicted relationships differ between the two versions.[8] Thus, I do not consider the theory to have an implication about either of these relationships. Ideally, however, I would include both variables in the empirical analyses since they appear in the formal model. I do include a measure of the balance of forces, but have no good measure of the costs of war.

Determining robustness is an art. One would like implications to hold across substantively equivalent equilibria, but there is no set method for determining which equilibria are substantively equivalent. Nevertheless, the robustness checks do have something to say about which implications of the model are really central. If the empirical results were to contradict implications 1 and 2, this would contradict the substance of the theory and make us question its usefulness. If they were to contradict the implications that I rule out as "not robust," this would not provide information useful for evaluating the theory.

Data and Methodology

This section describes how I use information about states' interactions to evaluate my theory. After noting my sources, I discuss the measurement of the steps of dispute escalation: threat, counter-threat, attack, and defense. I also discuss the measurement of concepts that I use to explain dispute escalation, focusing on the prime variable of interest, the defender's reputation for honesty. I then explain the statistical technique that I use to analyze this information, concluding with the main results.

Sources of Information

To examine the effects of reputations on the escalation of disputes, I use information from the Correlates of War (COW) project. These data, which are widely used to study international disputes and crises, include information about more than two hundred states over the course of almost 200 years.[9]

To measure the dependent variables, I use COW's Militarized International Dispute (MID) data set (Gochman and Maoz 1984; Jones, Bremer,

---

[8] In both cases, the relationships are nonlinear and difficult to summarize succinctly.

[9] In merging and manipulating the data, I used the helpful computer program *EUGene: Expected Utility Generation and Data Management Program* (version 2.10), created by Bennett and Stam (see Bennett and Stam 2000), and available at <http://www. eugenesoftware.org>.

and Singer 1996). The creators of the data set define a MID as an event in which at least one state took overt militarized action against another, where a militarized action may be as minor as a threat to use force or as major as a full-scale war (Jones et al. 1996, 168–77). The action in question must be taken by the official military forces or governmental representatives of a state. MIDs are quite varied in terms of the issues involved and the degree of force used; examples include the Falklands War and British efforts to stop the Brazilian slave trade (Jones et al. 1996, 178).

The data set contains information about each MID that occurred between the years 1816 and 1993. This complete coverage is crucial for evaluating the efficacy of diplomacy, since I must have information about each state's recent history of disputes in order to ascertain its reputation. I supplement these data with information about which pairs of states existed in the international system in a given year. These pairs, or "dyads," also had outcomes in these years, though these outcomes were non-events. (For example, neither state began a militarized dispute with the other.) I use all of these MIDs for the coding of reputations. However, because of the format of the MID data set, the same MID may appear several times if it is ongoing over several years. In order to avoid artificially inflating the number of independent observations in the data set, I use only the first year of an ongoing MID when I estimate the causes of dispute escalation.[10] In other words, I use only one observation per MID for estimation.

To measure the independent variables, I again use MID data, but supplemented by information from the COW National Capabilities data set. The National Capabilities data set contains information about the military capabilities of states that are not involved in disputes, as well as of those that are, and thus provides information relevant for investigating the initiation, as well as the progress, of disputes.

To test the implications of the theory, I identify one state in a dispute as "challenger" and the other as "defender." Several states may be involved in any international incident; however, each observation in the data set corresponds to one pair of states (dyad). Within a disputing pair, one state is on the side that initiated the dispute, and the other is a target. If there is a MID, I define the challenger as the state on the initiating side of the dispute and the defender as the state on the target side. In a year with no MID, any state could have initiated a dispute. Thus, in any year with no MID, each pair of states is represented by two observations,

---

[10] I include additional information about ongoing MIDs for purposes of coding reputations so that I do not mistakenly code a state as having a reputation for honesty because I have dropped information on its (ongoing) MID-year. After coding reputations, however, I keep additional observations based on an ongoing MID only if a state initiates a new dispute within a MID. When missing data and a few other issues also are taken into account, the analyses are based upon about 1,300 MIDs.

one with the first state listed as the (potential) challenger and the second as the (potential) defender, and the other with the states reversed.

The Dependent Variables: What Is Deterrence Success? What Does It Mean for the Defender to Follow Through on Its Threats?

The crucial implications of the theory concern two decisions. First, if the defender tries deterrence, does the challenger nevertheless decide to attack (resulting in a deterrence failure), or does it back down? Second, if the challenger decides to attack, does the defender follow through on its deterrent threat and fight, or does it back down? As I discuss later, one cannot investigate these decisions empirically without examining the decisions that are temporally prior to them in a dispute: the challenger's decision about whether or not to initiate a dispute, and the defender's decision about whether or not to try deterrence. Conceptually, these decisions result in four binary outcomes, corresponding to the four steps of a dispute that I discuss in chapter 3 (e.g., no threat by challenger/threat by challenger).

To measure these concepts, I use variables in the MID data set that describe the highest "hostility level" reached by each state in a dispute. The variables contain five possible hostility levels, ranging from the absence of militarized action to war.[11] If the challenger took an action that is at least as "hostile" as a threat to use force, I describe it as having threatened. Only if the challenger threatened do I code the variables that are temporally subsequent in a dispute. I describe the defender as having tried deterrence if that state, in turn, took an action that was at least as hostile as a threat to use force. Again, only if the defender threatened do I code the subsequent variables. I describe the challenger as having attacked if it used force and/or went to war. If the challenger attacked, I code the defender as having fought if it also used force and/or went to war. Table 4.1 shows this method of coding.

Though the MID data provide useful information for testing the theory, they are not perfect for my purpose. First, because the data set does not provide information about a state's actions prior to the one with the highest hostility level, one cannot know with certainty that a state that went to war threatened before doing so. Second, the data set does not contain information on the dates of dispute actions. For example, in a certain dispute, I might know that the defender's most hostile action was to threaten the use of force, while the challenger went so far as to use force. The data set does not reveal with certainty that the defender

---

[11] The hostility levels are (in increasing order): no militarized action, threat to use force, display of force, use of force, and war.

TABLE 4.1
Dispute Actions

	Value of Hostility-Level Variable	Coded Outcome
	chal. at least threatened	chal. threatened
Coded if chal. threatened:	def. at least threatened	def. threatened
Coded if def. threatened:	chal. at least used force	chal. attacked
Coded if chal. attacked:	def. at least used force	def. fought

tried deterrence and deterrence failed; it is possible, for example, that the defender threatened the use of force after the challenger attacked. I infer the actions that a state took prior to the one with the highest hostility level and the temporal progression of the dispute.

Note that if the progression of a dispute matches the broad outlines of my model, then the inferences that I make about the progression of the dispute (e.g., that the defender tried deterrence before fighting, if it fought) are correct. While it would be nice to test my theory using only cases that match it closely (cases to which it very clearly applies), the MID data are the best available for my purpose because of their in-depth coverage of all disputes in a time frame and the fact that they provide a lot of information about crisis behavior.[12] If the results of the data analyses were inconsistent with my theory, one might attribute this to the data being imperfect for the test (the inclusion of random noise). However, I find the patterns implied by my model in the MID data. It seems likely that if the inclusion of these other cases has any effect, it is to understate the importance of diplomacy in international disputes.

The Independent Variables: Reputations and the Military Balance

Having described how I measure outcomes, I now turn to the factors that influence the escalation of disputes. I discuss the factors that are important in the model—reputations and the military balance—followed by the issue of including control variables.

MEASURING REPUTATIONS

I use the four dependent variables described earlier to create a variable that describes a defender's reputation at the start of the present

---

[12] I do discard some cases based on the information in the MID data set. For example, I discard cases in which the state listed as being on the initiating side did not at least threaten the use of force but the state listed as being on the target side did so. I discard these cases because these facts strongly suggest, though they do not indicate definitively, that the initiating state was not really the challenger.

interaction. The four dependent variables together characterize five possible dispute outcomes: (1) there is no dispute (neither state becomes a challenger by threatening the use of force); or a dispute exists (one state threatens) and (2) the defender does not threaten (try deterrence); (3) the defender threatens and the challenger backs down; (4) the defender threatens, the challenger attacks, and the defender backs down; and (5) both states threaten and follow through on their threats to use force.

In the equilibrium discussed in chapter 3, a defender acquires a reputation for bluffing if it bluffs and is caught—that is, if it threatens, deterrence fails, and it backs down (outcome 4 in the previous paragraph). I define a state as increasing its reputation for bluffing in a given year if it is the defender in a dispute and this is the outcome.[13] As in the game-theoretic model, a state maintains a reputation for honesty in one of three ways. The first corresponds to the fading of a reputation: if a state is not involved in a dispute in a given year, it cannot acquire a reputation for bluffing; if it has such a reputation, it fades. The second is acquiescence: if a defender does not try deterrence (acquiesces), it maintains its reputation for honesty. The third is following through on its threats; if the defender tries deterrence and fights if deterrence fails, it maintains its reputation for honesty.

The theory implies that a state's reputation is temporary, but provides no other guidance as to the duration of a reputation for bluffing. In the formal analyses, a reputation for bluffing is binary: a state either has one or it does not. In the real world, memories of past events fade slowly over time; having been caught bluffing a few years in the past probably still affects a state's reputation today, but less so than having been caught bluffing a year ago. To incorporate the idea that memories of called bluffs fade over time, I define reputations in such a way that any called bluffs in the previous ten years add to a state's current reputation for bluffing, but a bluff farther in the past has less of an effect on today's reputation than one that is more recent.

Specifically, a particular called bluff in the past ten years adds $.85^\alpha$ to a state's reputation for bluffing, where α is the time passed since the bluff was called. Figure 4.1 shows the amount that a particular called bluff adds to a state's reputation for bluffing under this coding, where the number on the horizontal axis represents the number of years that have passed since the state was caught in that particular bluff. For example, if a defender bluffed and was caught in each of the previous two years,

---

[13] The defender acquires a reputation for bluffing in the equilibrium only if the challenger is listening—that is, only if it began the interaction with a reputation for honesty. I operationalize reputations more simply, designating a state as acquiring a reputation for bluffing whenever it is caught bluffing.

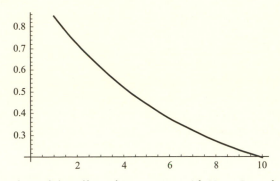

FIGURE 4.1. Coding of the Effect of Reputation with Years Passed

but not in the eight years prior to them, its reputation would be coded as $.85 + .85^2 = 1.5725$. The variable ranges from approximately zero to 3.83. In the discussion that follows, I sometimes refer to the effect of a defender having "a reputation for bluffing" or "a reputation for honesty." Since the reputation variable has many values, this terminology is technically incorrect. What I mean is that the defender has *more of* a reputation for bluffing or *more of* a reputation for honesty.

Moving from the formal model to empirical definitions of reputations requires some judgment calls. Later in the chapter, I explore the consequences of defining reputations differently. The first alternative definition is simpler: a defender's reputation is based on whether or not it was a defender in the previous year and, if so, if it was caught bluffing in that year. The second is more complicated: a defender's reputation is based upon past behavior when it was a challenger, in addition to its behavior when it was a defender.

MILITARY POWER

Like much of the literature on international crises, my theory implies that the balance of military capabilities affects the course of international disputes. However, the model does not have robust implications about the directions of the effects; slight perturbations of the model imply different relationships. Since the variable appears in the formal model, I include a measure of the balance of military capabilities between the challenger and the defender (or between the two states if there is no dispute) in the statistical model. Though the estimates are not tests of the theory, they do give potentially important information about the escalation of disputes. I base the measure of the military balance variable upon the National Capabilities Index, a composite indicator of a state's military strength (Singer, Bremer, and Stuckey 1972). This index, which ranges between zero and one, is based upon a state's fraction of the total capabilities in the international system in six areas: iron and steel production, military personnel, urban population, total population, military expenditures, and energy production.

Because the National Capabilities Index includes these six factors, it is primarily an index of latent capabilities. Rough calculations suggest that, on average, neither challengers' nor defenders' capabilities scores change much in the one to five years prior to a militarized international dispute.[14] One might think of using at least three types of measures of capabilities: latent capabilities, including resources like iron and steel that the state has not translated into military might, but could in the case of a war, as well as overtly military capabilities like military personnel; general capabilities, resources the state has translated into military might but are not necessarily at the site of a dispute; and immediate capabilities, resources that a state has translated into military might and moved to the site of a dispute. While Huth (1988) suggests that immediate capabilities, at the site of the dispute, are the most important to deterrence, the latent capabilities measure has an advantage for these analyses. Both general and immediate capabilities are more likely to be endogenous to the existence of a militarized dispute; a state that anticipates a crisis is likely to try to build up its military. Latent capabilities are more truly exogenous, and thus better can be used as an independent variable in the statistical analyses.

Most theories, including mine, suggest that the relative strength of the challenger and the defender affects the progression of a dispute.[15] To ascertain the impact of the challenger's relative military strength, I create a log difference of the two states' capabilities. The log accounts for the fact that a challenger 110 times as strong as the defender is not much more likely to attack than one 100 times as strong, but a challenger 10 times as strong is much more likely to attack than one of similar strength.

Realists have long debated whether states are more likely to become involved in disputes and to fight when they are evenly matched militarily (a situation of "power parity") or when one state is much stronger than the other; see, e.g., Bremer 1992; Weede 1976. While power parity is not a part of my theory, I verify that my results about reputations do not change when the equation includes a variable measuring

[14] For example, considering only challengers that were not involved in another militarized international dispute (MID) five years earlier (and so had no obvious reason to have engaged in a buildup at that time), the average challenger increased its capabilities in the five years prior to a MID by about .0006. The average capabilities score for challengers involved in disputes considered for these calculations was about .04. This amounts to less than a two percent increase in the five years prior to the MID.

[15] For example, see Huth (1988, 41).

power parity instead of one measuring the extent of the challenger's military advantage. Following Schultz (2001), I include a measure of parity that is the military strength of the weaker state divided by that of the stronger.

OTHER, IRRELEVANT VARIABLES?

It has become customary in statistical analyses of international relations to include a number of variables that are irrelevant to the theory being tested; these are "controls" suggested by competing or complementary theories. In this work, I take two approaches: I base most of my analyses on a simple statistical model that includes only the concepts of my theory. However, to convince readers who disagree with this method, I also report results from analyses that include control variables suggested by the literature on international crises.

The simpler model is the more informative. Including a long list of variables often is a substitute for careful thought about the factors implied by the theory. Moreover, these extra variables do not belong in the model; including them may mislead or confuse the researcher about their own "effects" and those of the explanatory variables of interest. For example, according to current practice, the debate among realists over the manner in which relative power influences dispute escalation would speak to including two variables relating to the military balance in the statistical analyses: one that measures the similarity of the two sides' military strength, and another that measures the extent to which one side is stronger. If the effect of having one side much stronger disappears when the parity variable is included, a researcher might conclude that it is parity, rather than relative strength, that affects the course of disputes. However, such a conclusion would be unwarranted since this exercise is nonsensical: it amounts to considering the effect of making one side stronger, holding fixed the extent to which the sides are evenly matched.

For these reasons and others, methodologists are beginning to question the use of the regression equation as a dumping ground for unwanted variables. Achen (2003) suggests "A Rule of Three" (ART): no more than three independent variables per equation (in the absence of formal theory that points to more). I initially include only those variables indicated by the theory in my statistical analyses. While I do consider a variation of the statistical model that includes power parity, I do so as a robustness check on the results about reputations, and do not include this variable and the balance of capabilities in the same equation.

After considering the simple version of the statistical model, the chapter explores two alternative specifications for the reader who is not convinced by ART. In the first alternative, I include several "controls": whether or not each state is a major power, according to Singer and Small's definition

(Singer and Small 1982, 44–5), whether or not the states are contiguous (either actually contiguous or across up to 12 miles of water), and whether or not both states in the pair are democracies. I include the power status and contiguity variables because previous studies suggest that major powers and/or neighbors more easily can go to war with each other or are more likely to interact and thus to become involved in disputes (Bremer 1992; Siverson and Starr 1990). I include the joint democracy variable because a large literature suggests that democracies are less likely to go to war with each other than nondemocracies are to go to war with each other and than democracies are to go to war with nondemocracies (e.g., Doyle 1983; Russett 1993; Rousseau, Gelpi, Reiter, and Huth 1996), though both the theoretical foundations and the empirical results on this subject are contested (e.g., Farber and Gowa 1995; Gowa 1999; Layne 1994).

Democracy is a difficult concept to define, and the literature on the democratic peace defines it in many different ways. I investigate the robustness of my results about reputations using a simple measure of joint democracy based on data from *Polity III: Regime Change and Political Authority* (Jaggers and Gurr 1995, 1996). Polity III contains a democracy index, created from four components: openness of executive recruitment, competitiveness of participation, competitiveness of executive recruitment, and legislative constraints on the executive. It also contains an autocracy index which contains these elements and the regulation of participation. As is fairly common in the literature (e.g., Rousseau et al. 1996), I create a single democracy scale for each state. I subtract the Polity III autocracy index from the democracy index, obtaining a variable that ranges between −10 and 10. I define a pair of states as jointly democratic if each has a score of seven or greater.

Estimation Technique

I analyze two sets of statistical models, each examining the effects of military power and of reputations for honesty and for bluffing on states' decisions about crisis escalation. In the underlying theoretical model, the independent variables affect how much the states value each option (their utilities from making various choices). In practice, we do not observe the states' utilities, but only their decisions. The challenger either attacks or does not; if attacked, the defender either follows through on its deterrent threat or backs down. I model each of these decisions with a probit type of model designed for such binary outcomes. I then translate the results into probabilities to ascertain the magnitudes of the effects.

The first statistical model, described in the following equation, represents the probability that the challenger decides to attack as an increasing function of a linear equation that includes the military balance and the defender's reputation:

Prob(challenger attacks | chal. threatens, def. tries deterrence)
$= F$(constant $+ \beta_1$ ln balance of forces
$+ \beta_2$ def.'s reputation for bluffing),

where the βs, here and later, are parameters to be estimated that relate the explanatory factors to the dependent variable, in this case challenger's decision to attack. I also investigate two variations on this model: (1) an analogous model that also includes the independent variables designated as controls: each state's status as a major or minor power, whether or not the states are contiguous, and whether or not the dyad is one with two democracies; and (2) an analogous model that includes the same control variables, but with power parity instead of the natural log of the military balance.

The second set of statistical models represents the decision that the defender decides to defend as an increasing function of a linear equation that includes the same explanatory factors. The simplest version of this model is:

Prob(defender defends | chal. threatens, def. tries deterrence,
chal. attacks) $= F$(constant $+ \beta_1$ ln balance of forces
$+ \beta_2$ def.'s reputation for bluffing).

I also investigate variations on this model that include the control variables.

In order to obtain accurate estimates of the effects of the observed explanatory factors—the balance of forces and the states' reputations for honesty or for bluffing—I must account for selection in the statistical model (Achen 1986). Selection bias is a common problem in situations like this one. When challengers decide whether or not to attack following defenders' attempts at deterrence, these are all challengers that have initiated crises by making a demand coupled with the threat of force. Such challengers have "selected in" to a dispute, and they are likely to have values of unobserved variables that differ from the values of challengers that did not "select in" (threaten to use force).[16] Similarly, defenders that decide whether or not to defend following deterrence failure are all defenders that have tried deterrence. Such defenders differ in unobserved ways from defenders that did not try deterrence. For this reason, ordinary probit estimates of the effects of independent variables on either state's decision to escalate an existing dispute are inaccurate (inconsistent).

---

[16] More technically, there are two underlying equations for each state, a selection equation and an outcome equation, and the error terms in these two equations are correlated.

More specifically, states' resolve affects their decisions about becoming involved in and escalating international disputes. Resolve is notoriously difficult to measure. Like other scholars, I do not include it in the equations that represent selection into the dispute and the later decisions about escalation; if I did, I could capture the concept only poorly.[17] Without a statistical technique that accounts for states' decisions to select into crises, my estimates would be misleading. For example, a challenger that is extremely disadvantaged militarily may threaten the use of force (select in) because it considers the issues at stake extremely important. Because it considers the dispute important, this challenger also will be likely to escalate. If selection is not taken into account by the statistical technique, the estimates will suggest that militarily disadvantaged states are more likely to escalate than is, in fact, the case.

From a mathematical point of view, resolve forms part of the error terms that influence states' decisions about selecting into the crisis and their later decisions about escalation. This makes it necessary to account for selection in the statistical model. Of course, even if one could measure resolve, the problem of selection bias would remain: some of the same small factors would influence both selection into disputes and the equations of interest, making ordinary probit estimates inaccurate (inconsistent).

To obtain accurate estimates of the effects of interest, I model the challenger's two decisions together and the defender's two decisions together. That is, I use one selection-probit model that represents both the challenger's decision about whether to threaten and its decision about whether to attack. I use another model that represents both the defender's decision about whether to threaten and its decision about whether to defend if attacked. Of course, disputes involve a second type of nonrandom selection: challengers select defenders, and vice versa. Accounting for even one stage of selection is complicated. Since I believe that a state's own decisions are more highly correlated than are its decisions and its opponent's, I account for self-selection in the statistical model.[18]

---

[17] I argued in chapter 3 that a main purpose of the defender's diplomacy is to communicate information about how important it considers the disputed issue. While the defender communicates some of this information in the course of the conflict, the adversary rarely learns the defender's value for the issues precisely; it merely learns whether or not the defender valued the issues enough to fight (and sometimes it does not even learn this fact). While historians and other analysts sometimes obtain more information ex post, even they rarely learn a state's value for the issue precisely. For this reason, it is impossible to measure the defender's value for the issues precisely.

[18] The two equations in the text show a state's decision as also conditional on prior choices made by the other state. This is true empirically and in the construction of the dependent variables; for example, the defender only decides whether to defend if the challenger attacks. Each statistical model represents only the decisions made by one state, however, since the

The commonly used Heckman selection model (Heckman 1974, 1976) requires that the explanatory variables differ in the two equations being considered.[19] Like many game-theoretic explanations, my theory of diplomacy posits that the same factors—in this case, reputations and the balance of forces—influence all decisions in the model.

I use a new estimator that is intended for a situation in which identical explanatory variables influence the two decisions, represented by dichotomous dependent variables (Sartori 2003). The new estimator is similar to the version of the Heckman model that represents dichotomous dependent variables (Dubin and Rivers 1990). However, it adds an assumption: that the unobserved factors that drive each of a state's two decisions are the same.[20] As I argue in Sartori (2003), this assumption tends to be reasonable (and more reasonable than identifying from functional form alone) when one believes that the two processes have the same causes, as they do in my theoretical model. Sartori (2003) shows through simulations that the estimator is better than the Heckman-type estimator when identical explanatory factors influence the two decisions, even when the assumption that the unobserved factors are identical is fairly inaccurate.

Selection Effects and Ex Ante Indicators of Resolve

Readers familiar with Fearon (1994b) may question how reputations for honesty can enhance deterrence when these reputations are known by both parties ex ante (at the start of the dispute). Fearon argues that challengers nonrandomly select into crises; they take into account information that they know at the beginning of a dispute in deciding whether or not to make a challenge. If the defender is known to be resolute, only the most motivated challengers will begin a crisis. Since these motivated challengers are hard to deter, deterrence may be more likely to *fail* when measures available ex ante indicate that the defender is highly resolved (the opposite result from what one might expect if one were to ignore

---

statistical model is a model of a state's utility (Sartori 2003). The first implication that I test concerns the challenger's response to a deterrent threat; if there is no threat, I drop the case for purposes of analyzing the challenger's decision. Similarly, the second implication concerns the defender's response to an attack after a deterrent threat; if there is no attack, I drop the case for purposes of analyzing the defender's decision.

[19] Technically, one can estimate the Heckman model with identical explanatory variables in both equations, but then the model is identified only by the nonlinearity inherent in the discrete-choice first stage. Thus, in practice, an exclusion restriction is required. The Heckman model assumes a continuous dependent variable, which also makes it a poor choice for these data, but Dubin and Rivers (1990) and Van de Ven and Van Praag (1981) create extensions for binary dependent variables.

[20] Technically, the estimator adds an identifying restriction: that the error term for an observation is the same in the selection equation and the outcome equation.

selection issues). That is, ex ante measures of a defender's resolve may be negatively correlated with deterrence success.

As I discuss more extensively in the next chapter, Fearon's argument does not suggest that a defender's high level of resolve *causes* challengers to attack. Rather, it suggests that if one does not correct for selection bias in the statistical analyses, ex ante measures of resolve will be negatively correlated with deterrence success. If one does model the selection process, as I do here, one should obtain a correct estimate of the causal effect. This is because selection models take into account the differences in the level of motivation between potential challengers that do not start crises and actual challengers that do. Thus, if selection is modeled correctly, ex ante measures of resolve can appear positively correlated with deterrence success.

Reputations for honesty are not ex ante indicators of resolve. The possession by the defender of a reputation for honesty is an ex ante indicator that the defender's diplomacy in the dispute is more likely to be honest and effective. It allows the challenger to learn new information in the course of the dispute from the defender's words and increases the defender's chances of successful deterrence. Forward-looking challengers may be less likely to challenge a defender that has a reputation for honesty (as we see in the next chapter), but the theory implies that the defender still will be more likely to deter an attack when it has a good reputation. Without an appropriate selection estimator, one may not find evidence that the defender's reputation for honesty increases the effectiveness of its deterrence, even if this is really the case. For reasons already noted, my selection estimator accounts for the defender's own decision to select into the dispute, but not for the fact that the challenger chooses the defender. I nevertheless do find evidence that the defender's threat is more effective when it has a reputation for honesty.

THE ESCALATION OF INTERNATIONAL DISPUTES: TESTS OF THE THEORY

This book is about the effectiveness of deterrence and diplomacy. I argue that diplomacy often is effective because states that bluff acquire reputations for bluffing, which hinder their ability to use diplomacy in the near future. To preserve their ability to use diplomacy, states bluff only rarely. Thus, most diplomacy is honest, and states can believe it. Since most diplomacy is credible, states often can use it to attain their foreign-policy goals.

This chapter uses empirical information about states' behavior in international disputes to determine whether or not this theory of diplomacy is an accurate or helpful explanation of international relations. I do so

TABLE 4.2
Percent of Time Challenger Attacks, by Defender's Reputation

		Challenger Attacks (Deterrence Fails)?	
		No	Yes
Def rep.	More honest (rep. for honesty)	15.0%	85.0%
	Less honest (rep. for bluffing)	21.2%	78.8%

by deriving two implications about the effect of the defender's reputation on states' decisions about escalating international disputes and then using empirical information to evaluate these implications. If the theory is helpful, then, on average, the defender's reputation will affect states' behavior in the ways that the theory implies.

In this section, I examine the escalation and de-escalation of international disputes to determine whether the implications of my theory are borne out in the data. I begin with cross-tabulations to provide some intuition about the data. I then present results from the statistical analyses.

The chapter does not discuss all of the results that the tables present. The next chapter discusses results pertaining to the initiation of disputes and to the balance of forces, while the appendix discusses results related to the control variables.

Raw Data

As a first look at the data, tables 4.2 and 4.3 present percentages based on cross-tabulations. For the tables, I separate defenders into two categories: those with more-honest values of the reputation variable (values less than or equal to .32, that is, reputations in less than the 90th percentile of the reputation variable), and those with less-honest values of the reputation variable (those in at least the 90th percentile of the reputation variable). Table 4.2 examines the percent of the time that a challenger attacks following a defender's attempt at deterrence, comparing the frequency for defenders with more-honest reputations to that with less-honest reputations. Table 4.3 examines the percent of the time that a defender fights if the challenger attacks, again comparing defenders with more-honest reputations to those with less-honest ones.

The tables show the pattern implied by the theory for the defender's behavior: the defender is more likely to defend when it has more of a reputation for honesty. They do not show the implied pattern for the challenger's behavior: contrary to what the model implies, the challenger is more likely to attack a defender with more of a reputation for honesty.

TABLE 4.3
Percent of Time Defender Fights If Attacked, by Defender's Reputation

		Defender Fights If Deterrence Fails?	
		No	Yes
Def rep.	More honest (rep. for honesty)	15.1%	84.9%
	Less honest (rep. for bluffing)	32.0%	68.0%

The cross-tabulations, however, do not take into account issues of non-random selection. A rough consideration of selection issues suggests that the possession by the defender of a reputation for bluffing is likely to be more positively related to the probability of deterrence failure than simple cross-tabulations or ordinary probit analysis of the challenger's decision to attack would indicate. Probit analysis shows that the challenger is more likely to threaten the use of force, initiating a militarized dispute, when either state has a reputation for bluffing. A challenger nevertheless may threaten the use of force when the defender has a reputation for honesty. However, it is only likely to do so when it has a high value of the error term—in particular, when it has a high value for the disputed issue. Thus, challengers are more likely to attack when defenders have reputations for honesty. This is not *because* the defenders have reputations for honesty, but because challengers are unlikely to threaten the use of force against these defenders unless they also consider the issue important. Defenders with reputations for honesty get attacked more often *despite* their reputations, because these defenders also have more resolute challengers.

The selection-probit estimator corrects for nonrandom selection. The results of this estimation therefore are likely to show that the association between the defender's reputation for bluffing and the challenger's probability of attacking following a deterrence attempt is more positive than the cross-tabulation would indicate. Similar logic suggests that the association between the defender's reputation for bluffing and the defender's probability of defending following a deterrence failure is more negative than the cross-tabulations would indicate.[21]

The Challenger's Decision: Does Deterrence Succeed?

Does the possession by the defender of a reputation for honesty increase its chances of deterring an attack? Is a defender with a reputation for honesty more likely to follow through on its threats if deterrence fails? The statistical results suggest that the answer to both questions is "yes."

---

[21] Probit estimation indicates that the defender is less likely to try deterrence when either state has a reputation for bluffing, though the effect is small.

Tables 4.4 and 4.6 display the major results, based on the estimation that takes nonrandom selection into account. Table 4.4 shows that the possession by the defender of a reputation for bluffing makes the challenger more likely to attack if deterrence fails—as the theory predicts. Table 4.6 shows that the possession by the defender of a reputation for bluffing makes the defender less likely to follow through on its threats—also as the theory predicts.

The first column of results in table 4.4 reports the estimated impacts of reputations and the military balance on the challenger's decisions to initiate a dispute and to attack following a deterrence attempt on the part of the defender. This is the equation implied by the theory. In this table and in table 4.6, the second columns of results show the estimates when I include control variables measuring whether or not the states are major powers, whether or not they are contiguous, and whether or not both states in the dyad are democracies. The third columns of results show the estimates when I include a measure of power parity instead of a measure of the balance of forces. As with probit or Heckman-probit estimates, the results must be translated into probabilities in order to be interpreted substantively. However, the signs of the coefficients represent the signs of the estimated effects and the standard errors show the precision of the estimates.

Table 4.4 shows that the possession by the defender of more of a reputation for bluffing has the effect that the theory implies: it increases the challenger's propensity to attack, or the chances of deterrence failure. The coefficient on the "reputation for bluffing" variable is positive; the standard error is small relative to the coefficient, indicating that one can be fairly confident that the true relationship is positive. The second column shows that the estimate is similar when I include control variables in the equation, though slightly smaller in magnitude. The third column shows that the estimate is similar if I include a measure of power parity instead of the balance-of-forces variable.

Because the table shows probit-type coefficients, the coefficients do not immediately reveal the substantive importance of the variables. Table 4.5 translates the coefficients into predicted probabilities to investigate the magnitude of the impact of the defender's reputation for bluffing on the challenger's decision to attack. The predicted probabilities in table 4.5 use the first set of estimates in table 4.4.[22]

In table 4.5, I perform a series of thought experiments: "How does variation in the defender's reputation affect the probability of an attack

[22] I include the predicted probabilities for purposes of illustrating the possible magnitudes of the effects; however, as with any probit estimates, the true probabilities also depend upon any unmeasured factors in the error terms.

TABLE 4.4
Influences on the Challenger's Decisions, to Threaten and to Attack

	Implication of the Theory (+ or −)	Equation Implied by the Theory	With Control Variables I	With Control Variables II
Issue a challenge?				
Constant (standard error)		−3.07 (.00911)	−3.34 (.0138)	−3.42 (.0173)
Ln capabilities ratio [−12,12] (challenger's/defender's)		.0175 (.00299)	.00865 (.00435)	—
Power parity		.319 (.0156)	—	.279 (.0344)
Defender's rep for bluffing [0,3.8]		—	.227 (.0192)	.236 (.0191)
Challenger is major power		—	.504 (.0275)	.558 (.0237)
Defender is major power		—	.385 (.0306)	.371 (.0273)
States are contiguous		—	1.09 (.0207)	1.06 (.0209)
Both are democracies		—	−.517 (.0576)	−.515 (.0577)
Attack, if threatened and defender counter-threatened?				
Constant (standard error)		−3.12 (.00980)	−3.36 (.0146)	−3.43 (.0180)
Ln capabilities ratio [−12,12]		.0136 (.00348)	.0129 (.00487)	—
Power parity (0,1)		—	—	.240 (.0373)
Defender's rep for bluffing	(+)	.288 (.0177)	.202 (.0211)	.205 (.0208)
Challenger is major power		—	.436 (.0294)	.501 (.0225)
Defender is major power		—	.397 (.0319)	.371 (.0282)
States are contiguous		—	1.03 (.0220)	1.02 (.0224)
Both are democracies		—	−.553 (.0655)	−.549 (.0655)
Sample Size		1050479/1337	1008216/1261	1014852/1281

TABLE 4.5
Relationship between Defender's Reputation and Deterrence Success or Failure

	Prob(Attack | Threatened) Defender Rep. Honesty Second Stage (%)	Prob(Attack | Threatened) Defender Rep. Bluffing Second Stage (%)	Change in Prob. of Deterrence Failure (%)
capabilities 1-to-1	60.3	82.2	21.9
capabilities 1.46-to-1	60.1	81.7	21.6
capabilities 7-to-1	59.1	80.3	21.2

by a challenger that is involved in a dispute, *holding fixed the proba-bility that a challenger becomes involved in a dispute?*" These thought experiments speak to the effect of the defender's reputation on the chal-lenger's decision to attack, assuming that a challenger with the specified features was randomly selected (correcting for selection bias). Each row of the table shows the effect for a different value of the balance of forces (challenger's/defender's). A military balance of 1.46-to-one in favor of the challenger is the median balance for states that become involved in disputes.

To perform these thought experiments, I hold the defender's reputa-tion constant in the equation that represents the challenger's decision to threaten the use of force and vary its reputation in the equation that rep-resents whether or not the challenger attacks (whether or not deterrence fails).[23] In the table, a reputation for bluffing means that a defender's reputation has a value of .32, so its reputation is less honest than those of 90 percent of defenders. While this may seem extreme, remember that a defender has a reputation for bluffing with value .85 if it was caught in a bluff in the previous year. (Note that one must read across the rows of the table because these are selection-corrected estimates. One cannot read down the columns of this table to see the effect of varying the balance of forces on deterrence success/failure.)[24]

The advantages of a reputation for honesty are substantial. A defender with a reputation for bluffing is more likely to experience deterrence fail-ure by about 21 or 22 percentage points. The effect is similar in magnitude

[23] For the thought experiment in this table, I assume that the defender has a reputation for bluffing when the challenger decides whether or not to threaten the use of force.

[24] To see the effect of varying the balance of forces, one must hold that variable fixed in the selection stage and vary it only in the outcome equation. I discuss this effect in the next chapter.

regardless of the challenger's military advantage. As the theory implies, a reputation for honesty helps the defender to deter an attack.

The Defender's Decision: Does Its Threat Turn Out to Be a Bluff?

Table 4.6 explains why challengers are more likely to attack when defenders have reputations for bluffing: defenders in that situation are less likely to fight if their deterrent threats fail to deter attacks. Again, the standard error is small relative to the coefficient on the defender's reputation, indicating that one can be fairly confident that the true relationship is positive. The second column of results shows that this result is robust to controlling for contiguity, major-power status, and bilateral democracy. The third column of results shows that it is robust to including a measure of power parity, instead of a measure of the balance of forces.

In table 4.7, I again perform a series of thought experiments. This time, I ask, "How does variation in the defender's reputation affect the probability that the defender fights if attacked, *holding fixed the probability that a defender tries deterrence in the first place?*" These thought experiments speak to the effect of the defender's reputation on its decision to follow through on its threats, should deterrence fail, assuming that a defender with the specified features was randomly selected (correcting for selection bias). Each row of the table shows the effect for a different value of the balance of forces.[25]

The defender's reputation again has a substantively large impact: a defender with a reputation for bluffing is more likely to back down from its deterrent threats by between 5.3 and 6.1 percentage points. The results again are substantively similar, regardless of the balance of forces. Thus, as the theory implies, defenders with reputations for honesty use diplomacy more carefully: they are less likely to back down once they have threatened the use of force.

ROBUSTNESS OF THE EMPIRICAL RESULTS

The earlier tables show that my conclusions are robust to one kind of change: the inclusion of several control variables suggested by the literature on international crises. The second column of each table (4.4 and 4.6) shows that the estimates are of the same sign, though slightly smaller in magnitude, when I control for the balance of forces, the status of each state as a major or minor power, whether or not the states are contiguous, and whether or not they are both democracies. The third columns

---

[25] Again, one cannot read down the columns of the table because of selection effects.

TABLE 4.6
Influences on the Defender's Decisions, to Try Deterrence and to Defend If Attacked

	Implication of the Theory (+ or −)	Equation Implied by the Theory	With Control Variables I	With Control Variables II
Try deterrence if challenger threatened?				
Constant (standard error)		.661 (.0405)	.792 (.0678)	.700 (.0724)
Ln capabilities ratio [−12,12] (challenger's/defender's)		−.123 (.0142)	−.0937 (.0203)	—
Power parity (0,1)		—	—	.0875 (.131)
Defender's rep for bluffing [0,3.8]		−.0815 (.0673)	−.0415 (.0758)	−.00849 (.0741)
Challenger is major power		—	−.363 (.0898)	−.602 (.0748)
Defender is major power		—	.0272 (.119)	.343 (.0986)
States are contiguous		—	.0179 (.0738)	.0452 (.0742)
Both are democracies		—	−.467 (.205)	−.506 (.206)
Fight if challenger threatened, deterrence tried and failed?				
Constant (standard error)		.303 (.0372)	.363 (.0634)	.277 (.0693)
Ln capabilities ratio [−12,12]		−.0725 (.0137)	−.0599 (.0194)	—
Power parity (0,1)		—	—	.203 (.123)
Defender's rep for bluffing	(−)	−.316 (.0624)	−.233 (.0687)	−.205 (.0676)
Challenger is major power		—	−.231 (.0870)	−.362 (.0720)
Defender is major power		—	−.120 (.109)	.0516 (.0894)
States are contiguous		—	.0829 (.0602)	.0742 (.0716)
Both are democracies		—	−.348 (.206)	−.314 (.208)
Sample Size		1562/1115	1476/1065	1476/1065

TABLE 4.7
Relationship between the Defender's Reputation and the Probability that the
Defender Follows Through on Its Threats

	Prob(Defend | Tried Deterrence Defender Rep. Honesty Second Stage (%)	*Prob(Defend | Tried Deterrence Defender Rep. Bluffing Second Stage (%)*	*Change in Prob of Defense (%)*
capabilities 1-to-1	84.0	78.7	−5.3
capabilities 1.46-to-1	87.2	81.8	−5.4
capabilities 7-to-1	86.3	80.2	−6.1

of these tables show that the results about reputations also are robust to including a measure of power parity rather than a measure of the balance of forces.[26]

In this section, I respond to three other possible criticisms of the results. First, one might question my method of measuring reputations for honesty and for bluffing and wonder if my results were an artifact of that method. I show that the conclusions remain the same if I use either of two alternative definitions. Second, one might posit that some states are more disputatious than others, and that my results merely capture this fact. I show that this alternative hypothesis is inconsistent with the data. Finally, one might wonder if my measure of reputations for honesty were capturing the effect of reputations for resolve. I show that my reputations variable affects the course of international interactions, even parsing out the overlap between the two concepts of reputations.

Alternative Measures of Reputations for Honesty

I first consider two alternative definitions of the defender's reputation for bluffing or for honesty. Earlier, I defined reputations in terms of whether or not the defender was caught bluffing in each of the previous ten years, with called bluffs discounted more the farther they are in the defender's past. Here, I consider robustness to two alternative definitions, one more simple and one more complicated. The first, and simpler, is: the defender has a reputation for bluffing if it was caught bluffing in the previous year (it tried deterrence, the challenger nevertheless attacked, and the defender backed down); otherwise, it has a reputation for honesty.

---

[26] See my earlier discussion of control variables for an explanation of why I do not include power parity and the balance of forces in the same specification.

The second definition includes behavior from previous disputes in which the present defender was a challenger as part of the basis of the defender's reputation. The formal analyses of chapter 3 argue that *defenders* obtain reputations for bluffing or for honesty, and defenders with reputations for honesty are able to use threats more effectively. The definition of the defender's reputation that I used earlier follows closely from these formal analyses. In practice, however, states clearly also do communicate when they are challengers. It is possible that states acquire reputations for honesty or for bluffing from interactions in which they are challengers as well as from those in which they are defenders. In fact, the Korean War case study suggested that this is the case. That is, like the Chinese Communists prior to the Korean War, a state may threaten to use force to change the status quo in its favor (it may issue a challenge), and then fail to follow through when a defender states that it is willing to fight. When it does not follow through, it is shown to be bluffing: it has said that it is willing to use force, but now indicates that it is unwilling to do so, or willing to do so only in the face of little or no resistance. Thus, behavior as a challenger may influence the reputation of a state that is currently a defender. In addition, though my formal work does not speak to this subject, it also is possible that the reputation of a current challenger affects the course of an international dispute.

In my second alternative definition of reputations, I still consider a state to increase its reputation for bluffing if it is caught bluffing when it is a defender. I now also consider a state to increase its reputation for bluffing in a given year if it is a challenger and it is revealed to be bluffing (it threatens the use of force; the defender indicates its willingness to fight, and the challenger backs down). I again code the reputations from a state's behavior over the previous ten years, with events farther in the past carrying less weight in the same way. However, I now code each state's reputation as based on all such behavior—regardless of whether the state is a challenger or a defender now and regardless of whether it was a challenger or a defender in a previous dispute. This leads to a reputations variable for the challenger and one for the defender, each ranging between 0 and 4.55.[27] In the statistical analyses that use this definition, I also include a variable that indicates the interaction between the two states' reputations. If the challenger's reputation does affect its ability to use diplomacy, one might expect each state's decisions to be different when both have severe reputations for bluffing than when only one has such a reputation.

---

[27] Since there are more ways to increase a reputation for bluffing by this method of coding, the maximum reputation value is higher than when I use the earlier definition.

TABLE 4.8
Relationship between the Defender's Reputation and Deterrence Success or
Failure, Military Balance One-to-One

	Prob(Attack | Threatened Defender Rep. Honesty Second Stage (%)	Prob(Attack | Threatened) Defender Rep. Bluffing Second Stage (%)	Change in Prob of Deterrence Failure (%)
result reported earlier	60.3	82.2	21.9
def.'s rep. based on behavior in past year	22.6	76.5	53.9
def.'s rep. based on behavior as chal. or def.	54.7	86.6	31.9

My overall conclusions are the same with either alternative specification. In each case, the estimated effects of the defender's reputation are
of the expected sign and quite precise. Tables 4.8 and 4.9 investigate the
magnitudes of the effects using predicted probabilities.

In table 4.8, I again perform thought experiments to answer the
question, "How does variation in the defender's reputation affect the
probability of an attack by a challenger that is involved in a dispute
(the probability that deterrence fails), *holding fixed the probability that a
challenger becomes involved in a dispute?*" Remember that this thought
experiment speaks to the effect of the defender's reputation on the
challenger's decision to attack, assuming that a challenger with the specified features was randomly selected (correcting for selection bias).[28]
In table 4.9, I perform analogous thought experiments to investigate the
effect of the defender's reputation on its own probability of following
through on its threats, should deterrence fail. In each thought experiment,
I assume that the balance of forces is one-to-one. In the thought experiments that involve the more-complicated alternative definition, I must
also hold the challenger's reputation constant. I assume that the challenger
has a reputation for honesty, but the change in predicted probability is
similar if the challenger has a reputation for bluffing. When the reputation is based upon the simpler definition, the variable has a value of
one if the defender has a reputation for bluffing. When I use the more
complicated reputation, a "reputation for bluffing" in the table signifies

[28] For the thought experiment, I again must hold the defender's reputation constant in
the selection equation. I assume that when deciding whether or not to try deterrence, the
defender has a reputation for bluffing.

TABLE 4.9
Relationship between the Defender's Reputation and the Defender's Decision to
Follow Through on Its Threats and Defend, Military Balance One-to-One

	Prob(Defend | Deterrence Failed) Defender Rep. Honesty Second Stage (%)	Prob(Defend | Deterrence Failed) Defender Rep. Bluffing Second Stage (%)	Change in Prob Defender Follows Through (%)
result reported used earlier	84.0	78.7	−5.3
def.'s rep. based on behavior in past year	88.0	68.9	−19.1
def.'s rep. based on behavior as chal. or def.	87.6	77.6	−10.0

that the defender's reputation is worse than those of 90 percent of other defenders.

The first row of each table shows the predicted probabilities using my original definition of the defender's reputation. The next two rows show that, using either alternative definition, the defender remains better able to deter an attack when it has a reputation for honesty. Similarly, using either alternative definition, the defender is more likely to follow through on its threats, should deterrence fail, when it has a reputation for honesty. Both effects appear greater in magnitude when I use either alternative definition of the defender's reputation. Thus, varying slightly the empirical definition of a reputation for honesty leads to conclusions that are basically the same.

Are Some Defenders Simply More Disputatious?

Some readers may posit an alternative explanation for my results: some defenders are simply more disputatious, and disputes in which these are involved are more likely to escalate toward war. A defender only obtains a reputation for bluffing if a previous dispute escalated to the point at which it could back down from threats. Perhaps these defenders possess a disputatiousness that leads challengers to attack them more often.

However, this alternative hypothesis is inconsistent with the defender's observed behavior. If it is defenders' disputatiousness, not their inability to use diplomacy, that leads challengers to attack more often when defenders have reputations for bluffing, then these defenders should be more likely to follow through on their threats should deterrence fail. The data show just the opposite: as my theory implies, these defenders are more likely to back down if deterrence fails.

TABLE 4.10
Dispute Outcomes and How They Affect Reputations for Honesty and for Resolve, in Theory

Outcome in Time t	Theoretical Effect on Rep. for Resolve in t+1	Theoretical Effect on Rep. for Honesty in t+1
1. Defender threatens and follows through	Increased	Increased
2. Defender has no dispute	No effect	Increased
3. Defender acquiesces	Decreased	Increased

Reputations for Honesty or Just Reputations for Resolve?

Some readers may be suspicious that my measures of reputations for honesty really are measures of reputations for resolve. As noted earlier, deterrence theorists argue that some states are simply more willing to fight than others, and that their willingness to fight is an enduring quality. One of the situations in which I argue states acquire reputations for honesty also is a situation in which deterrence theorists argue that they acquire reputations for resolve: a state acquires or increases a reputation for honesty if it follows through on its deterrent threats following deterrence failure. The two arguments are thus difficult to distinguish empirically.

However, these two arguments are not impossible to distinguish empirically. A state also can acquire or increase its reputation for honesty in two ways that do not coincide with a reputation for resolve: by having no dispute in a given year, in which case its reputation for bluffing fades, and by acquiescing to a challenger's demands. Neither of these outcomes should lead a state to acquire a reputation for resolve. According to the logic of deterrence theory, having no dispute in a given year would have no effect on a defender's reputation for resolve, since the defender did nothing to demonstrate its willingness or unwillingness to fight. Acquiescing to a challenger's demands should decrease the defender's reputation for resolve (make it appear less resolute), since the defender showed through its actions that it was unwilling to fight. (See table 4.10.)

The results that I presented earlier are consistent with the implications of my theory: a defender's reputation for honesty makes it more likely to deter an attack, but also more likely to fight if deterrence fails. As a check that these results do not merely capture the effect of reputations for resolve, I create two separate dichotomous "reputation for honesty" variables (table 4.11). The first, "Rep (honesty minus resolve)," measures

TABLE 4.11
Reputations Variables to Differentiate Resolve from Honesty

Variable	Value of 1 if	Captures
Rep honesty/resolve	Outcome is 1 in table 4.10	Rep. for resolve *or* rep. for honesty
Rep (honesty minus resolve)	Outcome is 2 or 3 in table 4.10	Rep. for honesty, possibly rep. for being *irresolute*

that part of reputation for honesty that has no overlap with a reputation for resolve. It measures reputations for honesty, "minus" that part of the reputation that also would lead to a reputation for resolve. "Rep (honesty minus resolve)," has a value of one if the present defender either acquiesced to a challenger's demands or was not involved in a dispute in the previous year; it has a value of zero otherwise. The second, "Rep honesty/resolve," measures that part of a reputation for honesty that also might lead a state to acquire a reputation for resolve: it has a value of one if the present defender tried deterrence and fought after deterrence failed in the previous year; it has a value of zero otherwise.[29]

If my theory is correct, a reputation for honesty acquired in any of the three ways should increase the defender's chances of deterrence success *and* increase the chances that it fights if deterrence fails. Thus, both of the dichotomous reputations variables should be negatively related to the probability that the challenger attacks if the defender tries deterrence, and positively related to the probability that the defender follows through on its threats if deterrence fails.

If deterrence theory's argument about reputations for resolve is correct, one would expect the variable "Rep honesty/resolve" to have a negative effect on the probability that the challenger attacks (a reputation for resolve should make deterrence success more likely), but the variable "Rep (honesty minus resolve)" to have a *positive* effect on deterrence failure. The "Rep (honesty minus resolve)" variable includes previous acquiescence, which should make a state appear less resolute and make deterrence success less likely, as well as the lack of a dispute, which should have little effect on today's dispute. Thus, if the "Rep (honesty minus resolve)" variable has a negative effect on the challenger's propensity to attack, that is evidence in favor of my theory and against deterrence theory's reputational arguments about resolve.

[29] The variable that indicates that a defender followed through on its threats also indicates that it either acquiesced to some other challenger or had no dispute with another potential challenger; in the sample, in any year in which a defender tried deterrence and followed through, it also acquiesced or had no dispute. (The reverse is not true.)

Since most discussions of reputations for resolve concern its effect on deterrence success or failure, I do not consider deterrence theory to lead to a hypothesis about the effect of the "Rep honesty/resolve," variable on the defender's decision to defend if deterrence fails. If deterrence theory has an implication on this subject, it probably is that a defender that has a reputation for resolve is more likely to defend. Since reputations are tied to underlying resolve in deterrence theory, a defender with a reputation for resolve is more likely to be resolute in future disputes as well as in the one in which it acquired its reputation. However, theorists are not united on this subject; Jervis (1997, 266–71) would suggest that a defender with a reputation for *lacking* resolve is more likely to defend since it is trying to rebuild its reputation.

If my reputational argument is correct, the specification that I used earlier is correct, and one that includes these two reputations variables is not quite appropriate, because it includes two proxy variables for the same concept—the defender's reputation for honesty.[30] Nevertheless, one might expect both reputations variables to have negative effects on deterrence failure, since they both are measures of reputations for honesty. One also might expect both reputations variables to have positive effects on the defender's decision to defend if deterrence fails, since a defender is more likely to follow through on its threats when it has a reputation for honesty.

I estimate the effects of these variables in a multivariate model as described earlier, correcting for nonrandom selection and including the natural log of the balance of forces in the equation. Both of these reputational variables have the effects implied by my theory, as table 4.12 shows. In the table, the second column shows the implication of deterrence theory's reputational argument, the third column shows the implication of my argument, and the fourth shows the estimated effect. (All results are corrected for selection bias, though the table does not show the selection estimates.) As the table shows, the challenger is less likely to attack a defender with either kind of reputation for honesty than a defender with a reputation for bluffing. A defender with either kind of reputation for honesty is more likely to follow through on its threats, as is predicted by my theory—and not by deterrence theory's reputational argument.

These findings show that reputations for honesty—as distinct from reputations for resolve—affect the course of international disputes. If reputations for honesty did not matter, one would not expect the "rep (honesty minus resolve)" variable to have a negative effect on deterrence failure. If anything, the reputations for resolve argument suggests that this variable

---

[30] Achen (1985) shows that including two proxies for the same concept in the same regression equation can result in an estimate with an incorrect sign if the variables are measured with error.

TABLE 4.12
Parsing Out Effects of Reputations for Honesty and for Resolve

	Implication of Deterrence Theory	Implication of Honesty Theory	Estimate
Does challenger attack (deterrence fail)?			
ln capabil. ratio	+		.0111 (.00506)
rep (honesty minus resolve)	+	−	−.639 (.047)
rep honesty/resolve	−	−	−.252 (.0541)
constant			−2.72 (.0436)
Sample Size			941501
Does defender defend if attacked?			
ln capabil. ratio	−		−.0741 (.0174)
rep (honesty minus resolve)	none or −	+	.0877 (.152)
rep honesty/resolve	none or +/−	+	.364 (.177)
constant			−.180 (.140)
Sample Size			858

should have a positive effect on deterrence failure; its posited effect on the effect on the defender's decision to fight if deterrence fails is unclear.

The findings do not show that reputations for resolve—as distinct from reputations for honesty—have an independent effect. The effects of the variable "rep honesty/resolve" can be explained by either theory because the "Rep resolve" variable captures situations that could lead to a reputation for resolve and could lead to a reputation for honesty. Moreover, one of the implications of the "reputations for resolve" argument is contradicted by the data: a challenger is less likely to attack a defender if that defender recently has acquiesced or had no dispute. Thus, the findings suggest either that both types of reputations affect the course of international disputes or that only reputations for honesty have an effect.

Some readers might argue that the variable "Rep (honesty minus resolve)" does capture some instances of reputations for resolve, contrary to my earlier argument. That is, a defender that has no dispute in the present period already is more likely to have a reputation for resolve; it may have no dispute because challengers hesitate to threaten a state that they consider resolute. While there are not enough cases to break the reputations variable down further, I have done one more check: I have operationalized reputations for honesty is such a way that a defender can have a reputation for honesty if it used diplomacy honestly in a previous dispute when it was a challenger. In this operationalization, a state that is, at present, a defender has more of a reputation for honesty if it was a potential challenger in its previous dispute and it chose not to threaten the use of force. This behavior does not indicate that the state is a resolute type. The results that I discuss here are robust to this alternative specification.

My robustness checks suggest that the defender's reputation for honesty matters, whether or not a reputation for resolve also does so. However, the results do not constitute definitive proof for at least two reasons. First, when I do include both in the same equation, the estimate of the effect of a reputation for honesty that comes from acquiescence or not having a dispute on the defender's decision to follow through on its threats is small and imprecise. The estimate suggests that the effect is positive, but does not show with much certainty that there is no effect. The estimate of the effect on the challenger's decision, however, is large and precise. Second, as I mentioned earlier, it is not really appropriate to test my theory using two proxy variables for reputations for honesty, rather than one variable that measures these reputations.

In sum, reputations for honesty and reputations for resolve are overlapping concepts and are therefore difficult to distinguish empirically. Nevertheless, the data suggest that my measure of reputations for honesty is capturing something different from deterrence theory's concept of reputations for resolve.

This work is not intended as a definitive test of the importance of reputations for resolve. As I argued in chapter 3, it is theoretically quite possible that states do acquire both types of reputations. More work remains to be done to empirically evaluate the importance of reputations for resolve.

The implications of the model that I discuss at the beginning of the chapter are borne out by the data, when I analyze the data in a number of different ways. The defender is more likely to succeed in deterring an attack, and more likely to follow through if deterrence fails, when it has a reputation for honesty. This result is quite robust to alternative specifications and is unlikely to be produced by two leading alternative explanations.

CONCLUSION

The empirical analyses in this chapter reveal two facts: when a state has a reputation for honesty, it is substantially more likely to attain deterrence success; when it has a reputation for bluffing, it is substantially more likely to back down if its threats fails to deter an attack. The second fact explains the first. Defenders' deterrent threats are more likely to succeed (challengers are less likely to attack after hearing them) when they have reputations for honesty precisely because defenders with reputations for honesty are more likely to mean what they say. Thus, as I suggested earlier, a reputation for honesty helps the defender to communicate that it is willing to fight, but this ability comes at a cost: the defender must actually be willing to fight more often if deterrence fails in order to obtain this greater credibility.

Earlier in this book, I argued that diplomacy often works because of the existence of reputations for bluffing and for honesty in the international system. States often use their diplomacy honestly in order to avoid reputations for bluffing. Because so much of diplomacy is honest, states often believe each other's diplomacy, so diplomacy can be an effective tool of state.

The empirical analyses in this chapter corroborate that states' decisions about escalating international disputes are influenced heavily by whether or not the defender recently has been seen as using its diplomacy honestly. This evidence suggests that the explanation of diplomacy this book provides is a useful one: diplomacy works, in part, because it is valuable; states have an incentive to use it honestly today in order to preserve their ability to use it in the future.

CHAPTER 5

The Broader Importance of Reputations for Honesty

THE PREVIOUS CHAPTER showed that this book's theory of diplomacy predicts patterns of behavior that occur in real international disputes. This match between the theory and the data increases confidence in the theory as an explanation of diplomacy.

While the previous chapter was concerned with "theory testing," this one evaluates the broader importance of reputations for honesty from an empirical perspective. It also studies the effect of the balance of forces on dispute escalation. The theory and the empirical tests in chapters 3 and 4 show that states' reputations for honesty have an important effect on their decisions about whether or not to escalate existing crises to war. The importance of reputations for honesty in dispute escalation raises the question of whether these reputations also influence states' decisions about becoming involved in crises in the first place: do they affect states' decisions about whether to threaten the use of force? This chapter provides evidence that the possession by the defender of a reputation for honesty does discourage a potential challenger from becoming an actual challenger, but suggests that the defender's reputation has little or no effect on the defender's decision to try deterrence.

As I explained in the introduction to this book, many realist and deterrence-theory arguments suggest that diplomacy is an extension of power. Diplomacy is superfluous for a strong or powerful state, which is likely to obtain its goals in any case. It is ineffective for a weak or powerless state. This chapter examines empirical results regarding the effect of the military balance on states' decisions about escalating international disputes, and asks the question of whether or not diplomacy has value-added beyond the military balance. Not surprisingly, the balance of forces does affect states' decisions about whether or not to start, join, and escalate international disputes. However, as my theory of diplomacy predicts, reputations for honesty affect states' decisions, even controlling for the effect of the military balance.

The previous chapter explained that I consider the theory's direct, testable implications to be about honesty and the escalation of disputes, not about states' decisions to become involved in disputes or about the military balance. For this reason, the empirical analyses in this chapter are not direct "tests" of whether or not this theory is a useful one for explaining diplomacy. They are nevertheless interesting in light of the theory.

The Effect of the Defender's Reputation on States' Decisions to Begin Militarized Disputes and to Attempt Deterrence

Does the possession by the defender of a reputation for honesty affect the probability that another state decides to threaten it with the use of force? Does it affect the probability that, if threatened, a defender tries to deter an attack with counter-threats of force? In the data I examine, the challenger is more likely to threaten a defender with more of a reputation for bluffing, and the defender's decision about whether or not to try deterrence is not very affected by its reputation.

The top half of table 4.4 shows estimates of the effect of the defender's reputation for honesty or for bluffing on a potential challenger's decision about whether or not to threaten the use of force to resolve some issue in its favor. The top half of table 4.6 shows estimates of the effects of the defender's reputation on whether or not to try deterrence if it is the subject of a challenge. Since these are again probit-type coefficients, they show only the sign and precision of the effects; I translate them into probabilities to evaluate their substantive significance.

I investigate the states' decisions to become involved in disputes in tables 5.1 and 5.2.[1] In each of these tables, a defender with a reputation for honesty has a value of zero on the reputation variable, and one with a reputation for bluffing has a value of .32, again signifying that its reputation is worse than that of 90 percent of other potential defenders. Remember that, while this seems like a large number, a defender has a reputation for bluffing of .85 if it was caught bluffing only in the previous year. Because challenges are rare events, the tables show both the change in percentage points and the percent change. (For example, a change from .01 percent to .02 percent represents a doubling of the probability of a threat, or a 100 percent change.) Note that, unlike in the earlier tables, the numbers in these tables are comparable across rows and down columns; since I am investigating each state's decision about whether or not to select in to a dispute, I do not need to correct for selection bias when calculating the predicted probabilities. To see the effect of a reputation for bluffing, one can read across the rows. To see the effect of the balance of forces, one can read down the columns.

The sample probabilities in the tables confirm that potential challengers are substantially more likely to become actual challengers of defenders

---

[1] These tables use the first column of estimates in tables 4.4 and 4.6.

TABLE 5.1
Relationship between the Defender's Reputation and the Challenger's Decision to
Threaten the Use of Force

	Prob Chall. Threatens the Use of Force, Def. Rep. Honesty (%)	Prob Chall. Threatens the Use of Force, Def. Rep. Bluffing (%)	Change in Prob of Threat (%)	% Change
capabilities 1-to-1	.107	.150	.043	40.1
capabilities 7-to-1	.120	.167	.047	39.2
change in prob				
threat	.013	.017		
% change	12.1	11.3		

with reputations for bluffing: a potential challenger is about 40 percent $\left(\frac{.043}{.107}\right)$ more likely to threaten the use of force when the defender has a reputation for bluffing than when it has a reputation for honesty. At the same time, however, defenders with reputations for bluffing are only slightly less likely to try deterrence than defenders with reputations for honesty, whether considered as a percentage-point change or as a percent change. In addition, the estimated coefficient for this latter effect is imprecise and becomes much smaller when control variables are included in the equation.

The previous chapter showed that the defender's reputation affects dispute escalation in two ways implied by the theory of diplomacy. Deterrence is more likely to fail when the defender has a reputation for bluffing, and the defender is more likely to follow through on its threats, if it does fail, when it has a reputation for honesty.

TABLE 5.2
Relationship between the Defender's Reputation and the Defender's Decision to
Threaten the Use of Force

	Prob Defender Tries Deterrence, Def. Rep. Honesty (%)	Prob Defender Tries Deterrence, Def. Rep. Bluffing (%)	Change in Prob of Threat (%)	% Change
capabilities 1-to-1	74.6	73.7	−.9	1.2
capabilities 7-to-1	66.3	66.1	−.02	.03
change in prob				
threat	−8.3	−7.6		
% change	11.1	10.3		

Tables 5.1 and 5.2 show that the defender's reputation has an additional effect: a potential challenger is substantially more likely to try to change the status quo by threatening the use of force when the defender has a reputation for bluffing. Perhaps potential challengers realize that defenders with reputations for bluffing are at a disadvantage, and challenge them more often because they are easy targets.

The result about the defender's decision to try deterrence is more puzzling. Since defenders are more likely to attain deterrence success when they have reputations for honesty, one might expect them to be more likely to try deterrence under this circumstance. This turns out not to be the case.

While the theory did not speak directly to the effect of states' reputations on their decisions to become involved in disputes, it did suggest that the defender's reputation for honesty or for bluffing is an important variable that helps to explain dispute escalation. The analyses here confirm the broader importance of the defender's reputation, but they also raise the question of why this variable has little or no effect on the defender's decision about whether or not to try to deter an attack.

One possible explanation for this result is that defenders with reputations for honesty are simply choosing more carefully when to try deterrence; they counter-threaten the use of force no more or less often than do states with reputations for bluffing, but they do so when they intend to follow through if deterrence fails.[2]

THE ROLE OF THE MILITARY BALANCE

What are the effects of the military balance on states' decisions to enter and escalate international crises? Table 4.4 and 4.6 in the previous chapter include estimates of these effects. They show that both challengers and defenders are more likely to threaten the use of force and to escalate crises when the balance of forces is more in their favor. The estimated effects of the balance of forces have the same sign when I include the control variables in the equation. Unlike with the reputations variable, however, the estimated effects of the military balance diminish substantially in magnitude when I include the controls. This change probably is due to the inclusion of the states' status as major or minor powers in the equation.

---

[2] Another possible explanation for the result is that those challengers that threaten defenders with reputations for honesty are particularly resolute; since challengers know that defenders with reputations for honesty are more likely to follow through on their deterrent threats, irresolute challengers tend to refrain from threatening such defenders. This explanation is not completely consistent with the data, however, since challengers are more likely to back down after threats from defenders that have reputations for honesty.

TABLE 5.3
Relationship between the Balance of Forces and the Probability that the Challenger
Attacks after Hearing a Deterrent Threat (Deterrence Fails)

	Prob(Attack | Def. Tried Deterrence Capabilities Ratio 1-1 Second Stage (%)	Prob(attack | Def. Tried Deterrence Capabilities Ratio 7-1 Second Stage (%)	Change in Prob of Attack (%)
def.'s rep. for honesty	82.6	90.4	7.8
def.'s rep. for bluffing	80.4	87.7	7.3

Since a large part of what constitutes being a major power is being militarily strong, the power-status variables may mop up the effect of the military balance, artificially diminishing it. In the analyses about the balance of forces that follow, I use the estimates that I obtain without the inclusion of controls.

Since the estimated effects of the military balance on dispute escalation are probit-type coefficients, one again must translate the coefficients into probabilities to see the magnitudes of the effects. Tables 5.1 and 5.2 investigate the magnitude of the effect of the defender's reputation on each state's decision about whether or not to threaten the use of force. I investigate a change from a hypothetical scenario in which the states are evenly matched to one in which the balance of forces is seven-to-one. I choose the seven-to-one ratio because this corresponds to the 75th percentile of the "lncap" variable. The challenger is about 11 or 12 percent more likely to threaten the use of force when it has a military advantage of seven-to-one than when the states are evenly matched. The defender is about 10 or 11 percent *less* likely to try deterrence when the challenger has such an advantage.

Tables 5.3 and 5.4 investigate the effect of the military balance on the challenger's decision to attack after hearing a deterrent threat, and on the defender's decision to follow through on its threat to fight if deterrence fails, *holding fixed the probability that a challenger/defender becomes involved in a dispute* (correcting for nonrandom selection). Remember that one cannot read down the columns because these are selection-corrected estimates. The challenger is more likely to attack when it is favored seven-to-one by the balance of forces by seven or eight percentage points (9 percent), compared to a situation in which the states are evenly matched. The defender is similarly *less* likely to fight by about seven or eight percentage points (again 9 percent) when the challenger is favored seven-to-one than when the states are evenly matched.

TABLE 5.4
Relationship between the Balance of Forces and the Probability that the Defender
Defends if Deterrence Fails

	Prob(Defender Fights |Chal. Attacks Capabilities Ratio 1-1 Second Stage (%)	Prob(Defender Fights |Chal. Attacks Capabilities Ratio 7-1 Second Stage (%)	Change in Prob Defender Fights (%)
def.'s rep. for honesty	84.7	77.2	−7.7
def.'s rep. for bluffing	80.3	72.6	−7.5

DISCUSSION

As I discuss in the introduction to this book, the military balance plays an important role in deterrence theory's explanation of crisis behavior. Many deterrence theorists argue, and many articles show empirically, that states are more likely to escalate international disputes when the military balance is more favorable since they are more likely to win if they go to war.[3]

My view is that the military balance affects the escalation of disputes, but that it cannot explain why states are able to change their opponent's minds about their resolve over the course of international disputes and crises. States are able to change each other's minds about their resolve using diplomacy, and they are able to do so, in part, because of the existence of reputations for honesty and for bluffing. A central fact that emerges from the empirical analyses is that reputations for honesty and for bluffing affect the progression of the international disputes, even controlling for the military balance.

The results about the military balance are also interesting for a second reason that is unrelated to my theory. Deterrence theory's argument about the effect of the balance of forces is very sensible. However, the resulting hypotheses have nevertheless been called into question by Fearon's work on selection effects in crisis interactions. Fearon (1994a) agrees with traditional deterrence theory that challengers will be more likely to threaten the use of force when the balance of forces is more favorable (insofar as they know that balance at the beginning of a dispute). However, he

[3] For example, Huth and Russett (1993) find that it is more likely to fail when the immediate balance of forces is more favorable to the challenger; Huth, Gelpi, and Bennett (1993) find that deterrence is more likely to fail when the conventional balance of forces is more favorable to the challenger; Wu (1990) adds two measures of the balance of forces into his expected-utility calculations and finds support for his model. This result is not uncontested within deterrence theory, however. For example, Maoz (1983) argues that dispute outcomes are related to the balance of resolve but not the balance of capabilities.

argues that challengers will be *less* likely to attack when the observable balance of forces is more favorable, and shows this to be the case using data from Huth and Russett (1988). The reason for this reversal in sign is nonrandom selection: only very motivated challengers will threaten a defender when the balance of forces is unfavorable, and these challengers will be more likely to proceed to attack.

In fact, Fearon's story is not as different from that of deterrence theorists as it at first appears. That is, Fearon does not argue that a more favorable balance of forces has the causal effect of discouraging challengers from attack. Rather, his argument concerns the observed relationship between the balance of forces and the challenger's decision. His logic suggests that, even though a more favorable balance of forces encourages challengers to attack, the observed relationship will be negative, because of unmeasured factors such as the challenger's motivation.

Note, however, that Fearon's argument only applies to estimates that are uncorrected for selection bias. Thus, if his argument is correct, the relationship between a more favorable military balance and the challenger's propensity to attack should appear negative when estimated with ordinary probit (uncorrected for selection bias), because the differential motivation of various challengers is affecting the results. However, the estimate should be positive when researchers use a selection estimator. Such an estimator isolates the *effect* of the military balance on the challenger's decision to attack, correcting for the differences in the error term that result from nonrandom selection (i.e., correcting for the differences in motivation that Fearon hypothesizes).

I find that both deterrence theorists and Fearon are correct about the balance of forces. Table 5.5 shows this comparison. As Fearon's logic suggests, the relationship between the balance of forces and the probability that the challenger attacks (deterrence fails) is negative—when I estimate using ordinary probit, which is subject to selection bias.[4] As Huth and others suggest, the effect of the balance of forces is positive—when I correct for selection bias.[5]

Thus, a balance of forces that is more favorable to the challenger makes deterrence more likely to fail. One qualification to this conclusion is in order, however. As I noted in the previous chapter, my analyses cannot determine which is really important, the effect of the balance of forces or that of power parity. When I include a measure of power parity instead

---

[4] Since ordinary probit is not a selection estimator, the top half of the table is empty in this column.

[5] Huth (1998, 139) also corrects for selection bias and finds that the challenger is more likely to escalate when the military balance is more favorable to it.

TABLE 5.5
Influences on the Challenger's Decisions, to Threaten and to Attack

	Ordinary Probit	Selection Probit
Issue a challenge?		
Constant (standard error)		−3.07 (.00911)
Ln capabilities ratio [−12,12]		
(challenger's/defender's)		.0175 (.00299)
Defender's rep for bluffing [0,3.8]		.319 (.0156)
Attack, if threatened and defender counter-threatened?		
Constant (standard error)	1.04 (.0472)	−3.12 (.00980)
Ln capabilities ratio	−.0317 (.0187)	.0136 (.00348)
Defender's rep for bluffing	−.202 (.0696)	.288 (.0177)
Sample Size	1337	1050479/1337

of the balance of forces in the equation, then increasing parity, instead, appears to positively affect crisis escalation.

In sum, the balance of forces appears to have a fairly large effect on each state's decision to threaten the use of force, though these results are not robust to alternative specifications. The military balance also appears to influence each state's decision about whether or not to follow through on its threats.

Conclusion

This chapter discusses two subjects: the effect of the defender's reputation for honesty on states' decisions to threaten the use of force, and the effect of the military balance on dispute initiation and escalation. My theory of diplomacy points to the defender's reputation for honesty or for bluffing as a key variable that influences the course of international disputes. I also argue that diplomacy is more than an extension of power.

Here, I find that the defender's reputation for honesty or for bluffing has a strong effect on potential challengers' decisions about whether or not to try to change the status quo by threatening the use of force. Challengers are much more likely to threaten defenders with reputations for bluffing. My theory suggests that defenders with reputations for honesty are better able to use diplomacy to attain their goals, an effect that was borne out by empirical analyses in the previous chapter. I speculate in this chapter that potential challengers recognize that defenders with reputations for bluffing are at a disadvantage, and challenge them more often because they are easy targets. The defender's decision about whether or not to try deterrence is largely unaffected by its reputation.

I also find that the military balance has a substantial effect on the escalation of disputes. A potential challenger is more likely to start a militarized dispute, and a defender is more likely to try to deter an attack, when the balance of forces is more favorable.

The results about the balance of forces also resolve an apparent disagreement in the literature on crisis behavior by showing both parties to be correct. As deterrence theory implies, the balance of forces has a substantial effect on each state's decision about whether or not to follow through on its threats. In particular, a challenger is more likely to attack (deterrence is more likely to fail) when the military balance is more favorable to the challenger. In keeping with arguments that Fearon (1994a) makes, however, this effect is apparent only when the estimation procedure takes into account nonrandom selection. With ordinary probit, it appears that the military balance and the challenger's propensity to attack are negatively related.

At the start of this book, I argued that diplomacy has value-added beyond the balance of forces in helping states to attain their goals. The statistical analyses in this and the preceding chapter show this to be the case. The military balance does affect the success of the defender's threats, and it does so in a predictable way. Nevertheless, the possession of a reputation for honesty helps both strong and weak defenders to use diplomacy to convey information to challengers in international disputes. Controlling for the balance of forces, the defender's reputation still has a substantively large effect on the challenger's decision to attack. When the defender has recently been using its diplomacy honestly, it is more likely to find deterrence success—regardless of whether it is strong or weak compared to its challenger.

PART IV

Conclusion

Conclusion

FEW SCHOLARS WOULD SAY that they are pessimistic about diplomacy, but many theories suggest otherwise. In particular, many realists and deterrence theorists argue that military might has a substantial influence on crisis behavior, and that diplomacy and deterrence work—but primarily for the strong, and much less for the weak. Their arguments suggest that diplomacy itself is either superfluous or ineffective.

This book explains when and why diplomacy has value beyond military strength in allowing states to attain their foreign-policy goals. To make this argument, I reconceptualize diplomacy and deterrence as forms of "cheap talk." In common parlance, cheap talk means "useless talk" or even "insincere talk," but both common sense and a large literature in economics indicate that talk can be an effective means of conveying information to a listener. As this book shows, this also is true of diplomacy.

My theory explains that deterrence—one form of diplomacy—works precisely because it is so valuable. When states are irresolute, they are tempted to bluff, but the possibility of acquiring a reputation for bluffing often deters a state from doing so. A state that has a reputation for bluffing is less able use deterrence to change an opponent's mind about crucial information in a dispute, and so is less likely to attain its goals. States' leaders often use their deterrent threats honestly in order to maintain their ability to use diplomacy in future disputes. They are more likely to concede less important issues and to have those issues that they consider most important decided in their favor.

In chapter 3, I showed the logic of this theory using a formal model of states' interactions in international disputes. The model is unusual; most formal models examine each dispute in isolation, while this one examines it in the context of a state's ongoing international interactions, assuming that tomorrow's interaction might be with a different adversary over a different issue. Examining international disputes in this context allowed me to study the development of reputations explicitly, while many other models assume their form or their existence.

The model has two central empirical implications about crisis escalation: First, because a state with a reputation for honesty has something to lose, it is more likely to defend following a deterrence failure than is a state with a reputation for bluffing. Second, because defenders are more likely to be honest when they have reputations for honesty, challengers are more likely to believe their threats. Thus, a state trying to deter an attack is more likely to succeed when it has a reputation for honesty.

Chapter 4 used information about a large number of historical disputes to test these implications. A typical defender with a reputation for honesty is roughly 5 percent more likely to follow through on its threats than a defender with a reputation for bluffing. A typical defender with a reputation for honesty is roughly 20 percent more likely to deter an attack than a defender with a reputation for bluffing.

The theory's implications are about the escalation of existing disputes; it does not speak directly to states' decisions to become involved in disputes in the first place. Nevertheless, the theory led to the discovery that reputations for honesty and for bluffing are an important variable for explaining international dispute behavior. An additional result in chapter 5 confirms the importance of such reputations: potential challengers are more likely to threaten the use of force against defenders that have reputations for bluffing. Since defenders with reputations for bluffing are likely to have less success later in the crisis, these challengers may be thinking ahead.

The empirical analyses confirmed that deterrent threats have value-added beyond the effect of the military balance. While the military balance does affect states' decisions about crisis escalation, the impacts of reputations for honesty and for bluffing remain, controlling for the balance of forces. Diplomacy is an effective tool by which states—whether weak or strong—convey information to adversaries and often attain their foreign-policy goals.

The fact that states behave in international disputes in patterns that theory describes suggests that the theory is a useful one. The peculiar pattern of behavior suggested by the theory—states with reputations for bluffing are *more* likely to be attacked but *less* likely to defend if attacked—is unlikely to have arisen by chance.

But is this a useful theory of diplomacy more broadly, or only a useful theory of deterrence? The introduction explained my intention to focus this study on deterrence, with the hope that understanding deterrence as a form of talk would be helpful in understanding the effectiveness of diplomacy more generally. A deterrent threat is a form of communication, a statement by leaders of one country that their country is willing to fight or take other action to prevent a challenger from taking something of value to the defender or obtaining some change that the defender opposes. Thus, my study of deterrence, broadly interpreted, is a theory of interstate communication.

The logic of the theory applies directly to diplomacy. Diplomacy works because it is so valuable. When they have something to hide, states sometimes are tempted to bluff, but the possibility of acquiring a reputation for bluffing often keeps a state from doing so. A state that has a reputation for bluffing is less able to communicate and less likely to attain its goals. States' leaders and diplomats often speak honestly in order to maintain their ability to use diplomacy in future disputes or negotiations. They are more likely to concede less-important issues and to have those issues that they consider most important decided in their favor.

As an example, consider the act of diplomatic protest. Diplomatic protest is a verbal expression of unhappiness with an official action or policy of another state. Few protests are of such salience that they are tabulated as deterrent events. Nevertheless, as one scholar notes, "it is also intrinsic to protest that it threatens one subtle sanction. Through the very fact of presenting its note, the protesting nation implies that the other nation's failure to redress or correct its reprehensible behavior cannot help but chill, in however slight a degree, the complaining country's friendship" (McKenna 1962, 21).

A diplomatic protest thus consists of a claim that a state cares enough about something that it is willing to cool its relations with another state if that state fails to correct is behavior. The state receiving the protest must attempt to discern whether or not this is true. My theory suggests that states will acquire reputations for bluffing if they use protest cavalierly—that is, if they protest, but fail to cool relations with the offending state if it does not meet their demands. If this happens, others are less likely to believe their diplomacy in the near future. My theory suggests that most protests will be honest—so that states that disregard them will, in fact, find themselves in a chilly climate.

Similar issues arise in the context of negotiations. Negotiators often have incentives to misrepresent information. For example, if a negotiating team falsely claims that its country is willing to make few concessions, then it may get a more favorable bargain. The negotiating partner might prefer to make major concessions than to arrive at no agreement. However, if the negotiating partner is itself prepared to concede little, then the bluffing state may back down and accept a less-favorable deal. My theory suggests that the state whose negotiators are caught bluffing will find its negotiations more difficult in the near future, since others will be less likely to believe their claims. However, it also suggests that negotiators will bluff only rarely; this explains why states are often able to make agreements based upon purely verbal and written negotiations.

On a more macro level, this theory might help to explain the functioning of alliances. The details of the formal model apply less directly to alliances, which involve promises, rather than threats. Nevertheless, the idea is similar. States have incentives to form alliances that they do not intend to fulfill. Forming an alliance can make a state better off by persuading opponents not to threaten the state or its ally. My work suggests that states might acquire reputations for bluffing, of a sort, when they renege on their alliance commitments, thereby reducing the credibility of their future commitments. To avoid these, states should fulfill most of their commitments, a pattern that we see in practice (Leeds 2004).

It is fairly straightforward to apply the theory to forms of diplomacy other than deterrence. However, further empirical study is needed before one confidently concludes that the theory helps to explain the many varieties of diplomacy. Such a study will need to address several questions that the present one does not tackle.

Who acquires a reputation? In my empirical work, I examined behavior at the state level. I found that others responded differently if a state had been caught bluffing recently than if it had not, and also that the state itself acted differently if it recently had been caught bluffing than if it had not. One instead could examine particular leaders' or diplomats' behavior, checking to see if others responded differently if an individual had been caught bluffing than if she or he had not. Most leaders feel a responsibility to uphold the treaties and other commitments made by their predecessors. Similarly, most diplomats feel a responsibility to uphold the commitments made by theirs. This responsibility may be partly moral, but they also are concerned about their countries' reputations. I conjecture that particular leaders' or diplomats' reputations are likely to be important only in rare cases.

A more-plausible alternative hypothesis is that regimes acquire reputations; when a state changes its type of regime, it acquires a fairly clean slate. For example, it would be surprising if the new Iraqi regime that takes office after the American invasion of Iraq were stuck with all of the reputations acquired by Saddam Hussein. I expect that a study that investigated this subject would find, in most cases, some continuity and some change from regime to regime. Thus, I would expect such a study to add nuance to my findings, rather than to negate them.

Are reputations specific to a particular form of diplomacy or diplomatic context? In this work, I study reputations acquired in international disputes and how they affect behavior in subsequent disputes. The fact that the empirical evidence is consistent with the theory's implications demonstrates that this has empirical basis. Nevertheless, one might ask questions about whether and when being caught bluffing in one realm of diplomacy affects the success of other forms of a state's diplomacy. For example, does reneging on an alliance commitment affect a state's ability to use deterrent threats?[1]

---

[1] This question is related to another interesting one that I address only indirectly: does behavior in one region of the world lead to a general reputation, or one that affects a state's future diplomacy only in that region? I find evidence of the effect of general reputations for

This book leaves open many additional, interesting questions. As I argued earlier, reputations for honesty differ from reputations for having resolve; for example, a state may acquire a reputation for honesty by honestly admitting that it is irresolute. If states do acquire both kinds of reputations, under what circumstances does particular behavior affect one or the other or both?

Readers sometimes ask me if this book has the message, "Honesty is the best policy." My reply is not quite so sanguine. Successful bluffs promise something for nothing, and bluffing occasionally is a state's best choice. However, this book shows that honesty is an alternative to military might as a means by which states can increase the credibility of their future diplomacy. A state may or may not get away with bluffing; the only way to maintain a reputation for honesty with certainty is to use diplomacy honestly. The book does have a message: diplomacy is an important tool, and those who wish to preserve its power should not cry wolf too often.

---

honesty, but do not test for regional effects. Studies of reputations for resolve suggest that such reputations are more likely to affect interactions with the same adversary. (See Huth 1997.) However, as I discuss in chapter 3, reputations for resolve rely on disputes being similar over time. Reputations for honesty do not, and so it is less likely that they are tied to particular adversaries.

PART V

Appendixes

Characterization of the Equilibrium

I characterize a perfect Bayesian equilibrium (PBE) of the game that is shown in figure A.1. Chapter 3 describes the broad outlines of the equilibrium, in which the defender's threats convey information to the challenger. For the definition of being "caught bluffing" and the actions observed in period t on the equilibrium path after which the defender begins time $t + 1$ with a reputation for honesty/bluffing in equilibrium, see pages 63 and 64. The values of j, l, m, m', o, and q in figure A.2 can be considered thresholds; for instance, a challenger with a value for the issues above the threshold o finds it optimal to attack in time t if the defender was caught bluffing in time $t - 1$ or $t - 2$. Figures A.1 and A.2 are similar to the figures in chapter 3, but provide additional information and present some of the information differently. The "h" listings in figure A.2 refer to the nodes in figure A.1. For example, if the defender was not caught bluffing in either of the previous two periods, the stage-game strategy of a challenger with type between 0 and j is to threaten at node h1, not to attack at node h3, and to attack at node h5. The parameter m' is relevant only off the equilibrium path; I discuss it later in this appendix.

To fully describe the equilibrium I outline in figure A.1 and the text, I additionally must specify beliefs, both on and off the equilibrium path, and additional actions off the equilibrium path.

I begin with on-the-equilibrium-path beliefs; these are simply the beliefs that the players must have if they update according to Bayes's rule:

1. The challenger believes at the beginning of each period t that $i_t^d \sim$ uniform [0, 1] and the defender believes at the beginning of each period t that $i_t^c \sim$ uniform[0, 1].

2. If the defender begins period t with a reputation for honesty:

    (a) If the challenger threatens, the defender believes after hearing the threat that the challenger's type is uniformly distributed between 0 and 1 (h2);[1]

    (b) If the defender says "will defend," the challenger then believes that the defender's type is uniformly distributed between l and 1 (h3);

    (c) If the defender says "won't defend," the challenger then believes that the defender's type is uniformly distributed between 0 and l (h5);

---

[1] The labels ("h1," etc.) refer to the node in the stage-game figure at which the relevant actor holds the beliefs.

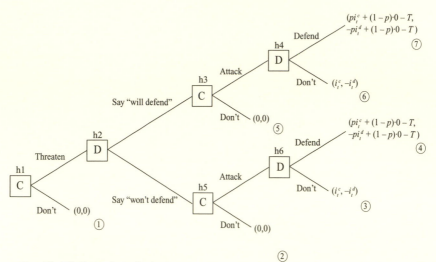

Payoffs: (Challenger's, Defender's)

C: Challenger's decision node
D: Defender's decision node
h1–h6: Decision nodes' labels

Parameters:
p: Probability with which the challenger is expected to win if war occurs.
T: Cost of fighting, which both states pay in case of war.
i_t^c, i_t^d: Challenger's and defender's values for the territory or other issues in this iteration, respectively. Note that the defender loses its value for the issue if it gives up through acquiescence, war, or backing down. In case of war, its expected value is $-pi_t^d - T$.

FIGURE A.1. The Stage Game, with Additional Labels

    (d) If the challenger attacks after the defender says "will defend," the defender then believes that the challenger's type is uniformly distributed between j and 1 (h4);

    (e) If the challenger attacks after the defender says "won't defend," the defender believes that the challenger's type is uniformly distributed between 0 and 1 (h6).

  3. If the defender begins period t with a reputation for bluffing:

    (a) If the challenger threatens, the defender believes after hearing the threat that the challenger's type is uniformly distributed between 0 and 1 (h2);

    (b) If the defender says "will defend," the challenger then believes the defender's type is uniformly distributed between 0 and 1 (h3);

    (c) If the challenger attacks, the defender then believes the challenger's type is uniformly distributed between o and 1 (h4, h6).

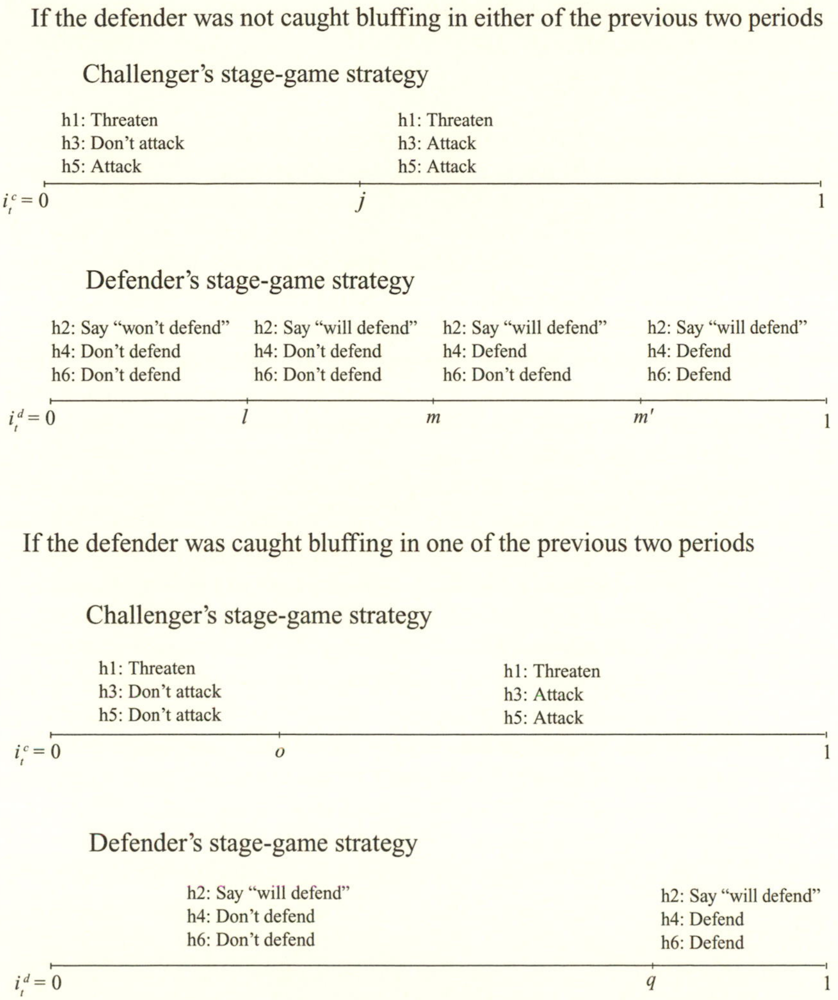

If the defender was not caught bluffing in either of the previous two periods

Challenger's stage-game strategy

h1: Threaten		h1: Threaten	
h3: Don't attack		h3: Attack	
h5: Attack		h5: Attack	

$i_t^c = 0$ _____ j _____ 1

Defender's stage-game strategy

h2: Say "won't defend"	h2: Say "will defend"	h2: Say "will defend"	h2: Say "will defend"
h4: Don't defend	h4: Don't defend	h4: Defend	h4: Defend
h6: Don't defend	h6: Don't defend	h6: Don't defend	h6: Defend

$i_t^d = 0$ _____ l _____ m _____ m' _____ 1

If the defender was caught bluffing in one of the previous two periods

Challenger's stage-game strategy

h1: Threaten		h1: Threaten
h3: Don't attack		h3: Attack
h5: Don't attack		h5: Attack

$i_t^c = 0$ _____ o _____ 1

Defender's stage-game strategy

h2: Say "will defend"		h2: Say "will defend"
h4: Don't defend		h4: Defend
h6: Don't defend		h6: Defend

$i_t^d = 0$ _____ q _____ 1

FIGURE A.2. Equilibrium Strategies, with Details

I specify additional off-the-equilibrium-path actions and beliefs as follows:[2]

1. If one or both players previously have been observed deviating from the equilibrium strategy, the challenger believes at the beginning of period t

---

[2] I explain the logic of the off-path actions and beliefs later in this appendix. Since each state receives a new type at the start of period $t + 1$, beliefs at the terminal node of the stage game are unimportant.

that $i_t^d \sim$ uniform$[0, 1]$ and the defender believes at the beginning of period t that $i_t^c \sim$ uniform$[0, 1]$.

2. If the defender begins period t with a reputation for honesty:

(a) If the challenger does not threaten, then the defender begins period $t + 1$ with a reputation for honesty; the defender and whichever challenger it is matched with play as in the top half of figure A.2 in that period;

(b) If the defender says "won't defend," the challenger attacks, and the defender defends, then the defender begins period $t + 1$ with a reputation for honesty; the defender and whichever challenger it is matched with play as in the top half of figure A.2 in that period;[3]

(c) If the defender says "won't defend" and the challenger does not attack, then the defender begins period $t + 1$ with a reputation for honesty; the defender and whichever challenger it is matched with play as in the top half of figure A.2 in that period.

3. If the defender begins the current period with a reputation for bluffing:

(a) If the challenger chooses not to threaten, then the defender begins period $t + 1$ with whatever reputation it would have had if the challenger had not deviated; the defender and whichever challenger it is matched with play in $t + 1$ accordingly;[4]

(b) If the defender says "won't defend," then the challenger believes in the current period (after hearing the statement) that $i^d \sim$ uniform$[0, 1]$; the defender begins period $t + 1$ with whatever reputation it would have had if it had not deviated; the defender and whichever challenger it is matched with play in $t + 1$ accordingly.

PBE is an extension of the concept of subgame-perfect equilibrium (SPE) to games of incomplete information. To show that the proposed equilibrium is perfect Bayesian, I must prove two things: first, that strategies are sequentially rational at every information set given beliefs, and second, that beliefs are consistent with Bayes's rule at every information set at which it applies. In the following few paragraphs, I provide an overview of the method that I use to show existence of this PBE. Basically, I use the ideas of the one-stage deviation principle and factorization and extend them slightly to account for the Bayesian nature of the game.

---

[3] There is another equilibrium of this game in which the defender receives a reputation for bluffing if it fights after having said "won't defend" (which only occurs off the equilibrium path). This equilibrium is identical on path; the solutions $\{j, l, m, o, q\}$ also are identical, but the off-path threshold m', described later, differs.

[4] Since reputations last for two periods in the posited equilibrium, when the defender begins period t with a reputation for bluffing, the reputation that it has in $t + 1$ depends upon whether period t is the first or second period of its reputation for bluffing.

To prove that a strategy profile S* is a subgame-perfect equilibrium of an infinitely repeated multistage game with observed actions, one can use the one-stage deviation principle (Fudenberg and Tirole 1992). One must verify only that no player strictly prefers to engage in a one-period deviation after any history, provided that the other players continue to play their equilibrium strategies. (The one-stage deviation principle applies if a game is continuous at infinity; this condition is automatically satisfied in a game such as this one with discounting and per-period payoffs that are uniformly bounded (Fudenberg and Tirole 1992, 108–110). For this to be true, I assume that the parameter T that represents the costs of war is bounded.)

To use the one-stage deviation principle, I begin by re-writing the equilibrium strategies and payoffs using the factorization technique developed by Abreu, Pearce, and Stacchetti (APS 1986, 1990).[5] Factorization is the Bellman principle applied to a game-theoretic model. APS show that after any t-period history, an SPE in pure strategies of an infinitely repeated game can be viewed as factorizable into two components: (a) its recommendation for play in the current time period t (its current recommendation); and (b) its recommendations for play from period $t + 1$ onward (its successor recommendations). I factorize the posited PBE in an analogous fashion.

To prove that the strategies in my proposed equilibrium are sequentially rational using the one-stage deviation principle, I must verify that: (1a) The challenger does not wish to deviate for one period when the defender begins period t with a reputation for honesty; (1b) The challenger does not wish to deviate for one period when the defender begins period t in the first period of having a reputation for bluffing; (1c) The challenger does not wish to deviate for one period when the defender begins period t in the second period of having a reputation for bluffing; (2a) The defender does not wish to deviate for one period when it begins period t with a reputation for honesty; (2b) The defender does not wish to deviate for one period when it begins period t in the first period of having a reputation for bluffing; (2c) The defender does not wish to deviate for one period when it begins period t in the second period of having a reputation for bluffing.

To prove that my proposed equilibrium is a PBE, I must additionally prove that beliefs are updated rationally according to Bayes's rule whenever possible, given the players' equilibrium strategies and that from each information set, the moving player's strategy maximizes its expected utility for the remainder of the game given its beliefs and both players' strategies (Gibbons 1992, 175–80). The only rational beliefs at the

---

[5] See also Stacchetti (1994).

beginning of t are that players are equally likely to have any type between zero and one. The equilibrium that I characterize specifies these beliefs and players optimize at the start of time t given these beliefs. It also is straightforward to check that beliefs are updated rationally within each iteration of the stage game since the initial distributions of types are uniform. Later, I check that strategies are sequentially rational given these beliefs, starting from each information set within the stage game after every history and continuing through the infinitely repeated game. For example, if the defender starts the present period with a reputation for honesty, the challenger threatens and the defender says "will defend," the challenger's beliefs at its next decision node must be updated according to Bayes's rule and its strategy from that node to time $t = \infty$ must be an optimal response, given these beliefs and the defender's strategy.

FACTORIZATION

I begin by using factorization to write the defender's expected payoffs from time t onward for arbitrary values of the thresholds j, l, m, m', o, and q. As I mentioned earlier, after any t-period history, any equilibrium must specify a successor equilibrium. An equilibrium can be factorized into the strategies it specifies for the current period, and the strategies it specifies from tomorrow onward. Thus, verifying that a player does not wish to deviate from the equilibrium strategies requires checking that it is not worthwhile to deviate once (today) given that the players play their equilibrium strategies from tomorrow onward and receive the associated expected utilities. In the equilibrium that I describe here, one must keep in mind that the successor strategies depend on today's play and there are thus two relevant continuation values for each player.

In particular, the defender's expected payoff from t onward depends on whether the defender was or was not caught bluffing in time $t - 1$ or $t - 2$. Call the discount factor δ, the total expected payoff from t onward for the defender who was not caught bluffing in $t - 1$ or $t - 2$ "w_1", and the total expected payoff from t onward for the defender who was caught bluffing in time $t - 1$, "w_2."

A defender who was caught bluffing in $t - 2$ has a separate expected payoff from t onward (and so a separate continuation value). However, as long as the defender has a reputation for bluffing, its choice of strategy does not influence its continuation value. Thus, the threshold for a defender who was caught bluffing in time $t - 2$ is just q (the same as for a defender who was caught bluffing in $t - 1$). Similarly, the challenger's threshold when the defender was caught bluffing in $t - 2$ is o. Therefore, once I have checked that states prefer their equilibrium strategies to all others when the defender was caught bluffing in $t - 1$, no additional calculations are necessary to show that players prefer their equilibrium strategies when the defender was caught bluffing in $t - 2$ instead.

Referring to figure A.2 for the meaning of the thresholds and the associated equilibrium strategies, the expected payoffs can be written as follows:

$$w_1 = \left[l\left(\frac{-l}{2} + \delta w_1\right) + (m - l)\left(j\delta w_1 + (1 - j)\left(\frac{-m - l}{2} + \delta w_2\right)\right) \right.$$
$$\left. + (1 - m)\left(\delta w_1 + (1 - j)\left(p\frac{-m - 1}{2} - T\right)\right) \right] \tag{A.1}$$

$$w_2 = \left[(1 + \delta)\left(q(1 - o)\left(\frac{-q}{2}\right) + (1 - q)(1 - o) \right.\right.$$
$$\left.\left. \times \left(p\frac{-q - 1}{2} - T\right)\right) + \delta^2 w_1 \right]. \tag{A.2}$$

To see the meaning of these value functions, consider the first term on the right-hand side of equation A.1: $l(\frac{-l}{2} + \delta w_1)$. The first part of this term, l, represents the probability that a defender that was not caught bluffing in $t - 1$ or $t - 2$ finds itself in time t with an issue value between 0 and l, since the distribution of values is uniform. The expression $(\frac{-l}{2} + \delta w_1)$ represents the ex ante expected payoff of a defender assuming that it finds itself with an issue value between 0 and l in the communicative situation; the payoff consists of such a defender's expected value today plus its expected continuation value. All defenders with issue values less than l say "won't defend," are attacked by all challengers, and give up the issues. Therefore, a defender in this situation receives a one-period payoff of $-i_t^d$; expected over its possible values for the issues, the one-period payoff of a defender between 0 and l is thus $\frac{-l}{2}$. Since defenders pursuing this strategy are never caught bluffing, their expected payoff from time $t + 1$ onward is w_1. In time t, this expected payoff is worth only δw_1. Of course, the term $l(\frac{-l}{2} + \delta w_1)$ represents only part of the defender's utility, the part that comes from those times that it cares about the issues an amount between 0 and l. The defender also expects that the interaction may be over issues worth between l and m or between m and 1, and assigns a probability to each of these possibilities. The remaining terms on the right-hand side of equation (A.1) represent the expected utility that comes from those possibilities.

In the work that follows, I first show that each player's choice of thresholds leads each player-type to prefer (at least weakly) the strategy it plays to a one-period deviation in which it plays the equilibrium stage-game strategy of a type falling into another interval between thresholds. The next paragraph shows that this is true if a type on the boundary is indifferent between the strategy to its left in figure A.2 and the strategy to its right in figure A.2. For example, when the defender begins the period with a reputation for honesty, the challenger's choice of thresholds leads each type of challenger to prefer the strategy it plays in equilibrium to the strategy played by a type in another interval as long as type j of challenger is indifferent between the two strategies in the top of figure A.2.

Define a player's strategy $\tilde{s}$ to be "higher" than strategy s' if both strategies are either in the top or in the bottom of figure A.2 and strategy $\tilde{s}$ is played by higher types in the posited equilibrium.

Remark 1. *For each pair of nonidentical strategies played by adjacent types in figure A.2 ("adjacent strategies"), one can show that the difference in expected utilities $EU[\tilde{s}] - EU[s']$ is increasing in the player's type, i, if $\tilde{s}$ is higher than s'.*

Thus, when each type on a threshold is indifferent between the strategy played by types immediately below and above it, no type wishes to switch to the stage-game strategy played by a higher or lower type.[6] If strategy $\tilde{s}$ is higher than strategy s' and a player of type τ is indifferent between $\tilde{s}$ and s', then all types smaller than τ will prefer s' and all types greater than τ will prefer $\tilde{s}$. Moreover, if types l and m are indifferent between the strategies to the left and right of them in the figure when the defender has a reputation for honesty, types smaller than l prefer their strategy to that played by types greater than m and vice versa.

Since a player learns its own type before acting in this game, each state's equilibrium strategy must be rational for a state ex post—after it learns its type—regardless of its type. For this game, there are two equivalent ways to derive the same set of equations that characterize the equilibrium. One can directly investigate which strategies maximize utility ex post, or one can find the strategies that maximize the two states' value functions. In this appendix, I directly investigate which strategies maximize utility ex post, though this method is more cumbersome, because I believe it to be more intuitive for more readers.[7]

After showing that each type of player prefers its own strategy to each strategy that another type plays in equilibrium, I check that no challenger or defender wishes to deviate to a strategy that no type plays in equilibrium. Finally, in order to verify that the equilibrium is Perfect Bayesian, I check that no challenger or defender wishes to deviate at a node other

---

[6] In all of the work that follows, I am checking that no player-type wishes to engage in a one-period deviation; thus, when I refer to a player not wishing to switch strategies, I mean that it does not wish to switch stage-game strategies, given that all players will play their equilibrium strategies from time $t + 1$ onward.

[7] The other method follows the logic of dynamic programming: maximize w_1, and w_2 and solve the resulting system of equations.

than its first node within the stage game after any history and then resume playing its equilibrium strategy in $t+1$.

Choosing Thresholds so that Each Player-Type Prefers Its Equilibrium Strategy to Other Strategies Played in Equilibrium

In equilibrium, each type of each state must play the strategy that maximizes its expected utility from the current node and time onward. For example, if the defender enters time t and was not caught bluffing in $t-1$ or $t-2$, for l to be an equilibrium threshold, type l must be indifferent between the two relevant strategies in figure A.2, assuming that the challenger plays its equilibrium strategy. If the challenger plays its equilibrium strategy, all types of challenger will attack defenders who say "won't defend" and only challengers with types greater than j will attack defenders who say "will defend." Thus, if the defender says "won't defend" and doesn't defend, then this defender always loses the issue but begins the next period with a reputation for honesty. The defender's expected payoff is thus $-i_t^d + \delta w_1$. If the defender instead says "will defend" but plans not to defend if the challenger attacks, then j of the time the defender gets away with its bluff and receives $0 + \delta w_1$. The rest of the time, the challenger is of type greater than j and calls the defender's bluff; the defender backs down and receives a reputation for bluffing, for an expected payoff of $-i_t^d + \delta w_2$.

For this reason, a defender of type l is indifferent between these two strategies when the following equation is satisfied:

$$-l + \delta w_1 = j\delta w_1 + (1-j)(-l + \delta w_2). \tag{A.3}$$

One can show in an analogous fashion that the other thresholds (m, j, o, and q) must satisfy the equations that follow. The challenger's choice of thresholds is theoretically similar; however, in practice, the problem is simpler because the challenger's actions today do not affect its continuation values. If the defender was caught bluffing in time $t-1$ or $t-2$, neither state's choices affect its continuation value so that each state's choice of thresholds is simple. The resulting equations are:

$$-m + \delta w_2 = -pm - T + \delta w_1. \tag{A.4}$$

$$j = \frac{(1-m)T}{m - l + p - mp}. \tag{A.5}$$

$$q = \frac{T}{1-p} \tag{A.6}$$

$$o = \frac{-T^2 - pT + T}{-p^2 + p - pT + T}. \tag{A.7}$$

The value-function equations, equations A.1 and A.2, and the five threshold equations, equations A.3 through A.7, constitute a set of seven equations and seven unknowns and characterize the strategies played on the equilibrium path.[8] In combination, these equations are highly non-linear. (For example, the equations can be reduced to characterize one threshold, m, with all other endogenous variables eliminated. This equation is very lengthy and I do not present it here.) I solve the system of equations numerically; each numerical solution is a set of values for the parameters, $\{j, l, m, o, q, w_1, w_2\}$, where the values satisfy the seven equations. To do so, I assume that the discount factor is 0.9. The numerical work shows that the equilibrium exists for many pairs of the exogenous variables T and p, since the equations can be satisfied by meaningful values of the parameters (values for which thresholds are between 0 and 1 and $l < m$). Some pairs $\{T, p\}$ lead only to solutions of the system of equations such that one or more states choose threshold values outside of the interval (0, 1) and/or choose $l \geq m$, so that an equilibrium of the posited form does not exist for these pairs. Table A.1 provides several sample equilibria.

The thresholds in the table are rounded to the nearest percentage (except .005, because zero would be a case of nonexistence for the interior equilibrium). As I discuss later, I use the complete set of numerical equilibria to determine implications of the model. For example, if a defender threatens, the threat is more likely to be successful when the defender has a reputation for honesty than when it has a reputation for bluffing (because $o < j$). When I refer later to situations in which a solution exists, I mean a solution with thresholds in (0, 1) with $l < m$.

TABLE A.1
Sample Equilibrium Points

T	p	j	l	m	o	$q = m'$
.1	.3	.22	.005	.14	.21	.14
.1	.4	.21	.06	.14	.17	.17
.1	.5	.19	.11	.15	.13	.2
.1	.6	.16	.16	.17	.11	.25
.4	.3	.28	.04	.55	.24	.57
.4	.4	.29	.14	.57	.17	.67
.4	.5	.31	.25	.58	.09	.80

[8] As I discuss later, an eighth equation characterizes the off-path threshold: $m' = q$.

CHECKING THAT NO PLAYER PREFERS TO DEVIATE TO A STRATEGY NO TYPE PLAYS IN EQUILIBRIUM

When the Defender Has a Reputation for Honesty

NO DEFENDER WISHES TO DEVIATE TO A STRATEGY NO TYPE PLAYS IN EQUILIBRIUM

When the defender has a reputation for honesty, there are four strategies restricted to the stage game that no type of defender plays in equilibrium.[9]

The first such strategy is to say "will defend," not to defend if attacked after having said "will defend," but to defend if attacked after having said "won't defend." The defender's action after having said "won't defend" does not affect its payoff, since it always says "will defend" if it plays this strategy. The earlier discussion of equilibrium thresholds shows that players with types less than or equal to l prefer not to defend if attacked after having said "will defend"; these player-types are indifferent between their equilibrium strategy and this one that specifies an alternative off-path action. Players with types greater than l prefer to defend if attacked after having said "will defend"; these player-types strictly prefer their equilibrium strategy to this alternative.

The second such strategy is to say "won't defend," but defend if attacked after having said either "will defend" or "won't defend." I begin by calculating the expected utility of a defender who engages in a one-period deviation to this stage-game strategy, $s^\#$. If it hears a defender with a reputation for honesty say "won't defend," the challenger's equilibrium strategy is to attack regardless of its own type. The equilibrium specifies that the defender begins the next period with a reputation for honesty if it then defends. Thus, a defender's expected payoff from this strategy $s^\#$ is

$$EU[s^\#] = -pi_t^d - T + \delta w_1. \tag{A.8}$$

Now I compare the defender's expected utility from this deviation to the expected utility of each type in equilibrium. No type of defender with a reputation for honesty gets a payoff this low in equilibrium. Intuitively, a defender can always do better by saying "will defend" if it is willing to fight, since this deters some challengers. More technically, if it plays its equilibrium strategy, a defender with a type $i_t^d < l$ always loses the issue, but starts the next period with a reputation for honesty. Its payoff is $-i_t^d + \delta w_1$. When a solution to the system of seven equations presented earlier exists, then a defender with type $i_t^d < l$ prefers its equilibrium strategy s^* to all other strategies that are played by some type in equilibrium, including

[9] See footnote 6.

the strategy of saying "will defend" and defending if attacked.[10] Call this strategy $s^\$$. For a defender with $i_t^d < l$,

$$EU[s^*] \equiv -i_t^d + \delta w_1 > (1-j)(-pi_t^d - T) + \delta w_1 \equiv EU[s^\$]. \quad (A.9)$$

Since $j < 1$ and $-pi_t^d - T < 0$, equations A.8 and A.9 imply that

$$EU[s^*] > EU[s^\$] \geq EU[s^\#] \; \forall \; i_t^d < l.$$

Similarly, since types with $l < i_t^d < m$ prefer their equilibrium strategy to saying "will defend" and defending if attacked to $s^\$$, they too prefer their equilibrium strategy to $s^\#$. Finally, types with $i_t^d > m$ pursue $s^\$$ in equilibrium and so prefer their equilibrium strategy to $s^\#$.

The third such strategy is to say "won't defend" and to defend only if attacked after having said "will defend." Again, if it hears a defender with a reputation for honesty say "won't defend," the challenger's equilibrium strategy is to attack regardless of the challenger's own type. The equilibrium specifies that the defender begins the next period with a reputation for honesty if it then defends. Thus, a defender's expected payoff from this strategy $s^{\#\#}$ is

$$EU[s^{\#\#}] = -i_t^d + \delta w_1. \quad (A.10)$$

If they play their equilibrium strategies, defenders with types less than or equal to l receive exactly the same expected utility, so they weakly prefer their equilibrium strategy to this one-period deviation. Defenders with types greater than l prefer their equilibrium strategies to those of types less than or equal to l, so they also prefer their equilibrium strategies to this one.

The fourth such strategy is to say "won't defend" and to defend only if attacked after having said "won't defend." The defender's expected utility if it pursues this strategy is given by equation A.8. I have already shown that all types of defender at least weakly prefer their equilibrium strategies to this one in this situation.

NO CHALLENGER WISHES TO DEVIATE TO A STRATEGY NO TYPE
PLAYS IN EQUILIBRIUM

In each of the following scenarios, the deviation that the state is considering leads to the same continuation value that the state will receive if it plays its equilibrium strategy. Thus, to determine that the state will not deviate, it is sufficient to check that the possible deviation would not increase the state's one-period payoff.

---

[10] When I refer here and later to the existence of a solution to the system of equations, I mean the existence of a solution with all parameters within the range of $(0, 1)$ and $l < m$.

When the defender has a reputation for honesty, there are six strategies restricted to the stage game that no type of challenger plays in equilibrium.

The first four such strategies involve not threatening. The fifth involves threatening but never attacking. If the defender plays its equilibrium strategy and the challenger does not threaten, the challenger receives a payoff of zero today. If the challenger threatens and never attacks, it again receives a payoff of zero today. Thus, for the challenger to prefer its equilibrium strategy to both of these alternatives, each type of challenger must receive a weakly positive payoff from the strategy it plays in equilibrium. If they pursue their equilibrium strategy, challengers with types between 0 and j receive $l i_t^c$; this is at its minimum when $i_t^c = 0$. Thus, challengers with type $i_t^c = 0$ weakly prefer their equilibrium strategy and challengers with types $i_t^c \in (0, j)$ strictly prefer their equilibrium strategy to any strategy that gives an expected payoff of 0. Challengers with types between j and 1 prefer their equilibrium strategy to that of types $i_t^c \in (0, j)$, so they must also prefer it to not threatening and to threatening but never attacking.

The last strategy that the challenger might pursue that no type plays in equilibrium is to threaten and then attack if and only if the defender says "will defend." Call this strategy s'. If the challenger deviates to this strategy, it receives $(m - l)i_t^c + (1 - m)(p i_t^c - T)$ today in expectation.

I compare this expected utility to that of each type if the type plays its equilibrium strategy. If a challenger of type $i_t^c \leq j$ plays its equilibrium strategy, it receives $l i_t^c$ today. We know that these types of challenger prefer their equilibrium strategy to that pursued in equilibrium by challengers with types $j \leq i_t^c < 1$. Thus, for these types,

$$l i_t^c \geq l i_t^c + (m - l)i_t^c + (1 - m)(p i_t^c - T).$$

Since

$$l i_t^c + (m - l)i_t^c + (1 - m)(p i_t^c - T) \geq (m - l)i_t^c + (1 - m)(p i_t^c - T) = EU[s'], \forall i_t^c$$

these types of challenger prefer their equilibrium strategy to s'. A type with $i_t^c \geq j$ receives $l i_t^c + (m - l)i_t^c + (1 - m)(p i_t^c - T)$ in equilibrium (with $i_t^c = j$), so it also prefers its equilibrium strategy to this deviation.

When the Defender Has a Reputation for Bluffing

NO DEFENDER WISHES TO DEVIATE TO A STRATEGY NO TYPE PLAYS IN EQUILIBRIUM

When the defender has a reputation for bluffing, there are six strategies restricted to the stage game that no type of defender plays in equilibrium.

The first four involve not threatening. It is easy to see that the defender cannot benefit from changing its message when it has a reputation for bluffing; its message has no effect on the challenger's actions either on or off the equilibrium path. I have already checked that each defender-type prefers its later action (defending or not if attacked) to the alternative; thus, each defender-type at least weakly prefers its equilibrium strategy to the four strategies that involve not threatening.

The fifth such strategy is to say "will defend" and then defend only if the challenger attacks after the defender said "will defend." If the defender plays either its equilibrium strategy or this alternative, it always says "will defend" and its action after "won't defend" does not affect its expected payoff. Defenders of type greater than q receive the same expected utility with this deviation as they do with their equilibrium strategies, and defenders of type less than q prefer their equilibrium strategy of not defending after saying they will.

The last such strategy is to say "will defend" and then defend only if the challenger attacks after the defender said "won't defend." Again, the defender's action after "won't defend" does not affect its expected payoff. Defenders of type less than q receive the same expected utility with this deviation as they do with their equilibrium strategies, and defenders of type greater than q prefer their equilibrium strategy of defending after saying they will.

NO CHALLENGER WISHES TO DEVIATE TO A STRATEGY NO TYPE
PLAYS IN EQUILIBRIUM

When the defender has a reputation for bluffing, there are six strategies restricted to the stage game that no type of challenger plays in equilibrium. The first four involve not threatening. If the challenger does not threaten, it receives a one-period payoff of zero. In equilibrium, a challenger with type $i_t^c \leq o$ receives zero, and so weakly prefers its equilibrium strategy. A challenger with type $i_t^c \geq o$ receives $q i_t^c + (1-q)(p i_t^c - T)$. This quantity must be positive for types $i_t^c > o$ for the solution to the system of equations to exist with $o < 1$; otherwise, types with $i_t^c > o$ would deviate to the strategy played by types $i_t^c < o$.

The fifth such strategy is to threaten but attack if and only if the defender says "won't defend." If the challenger deviates to this strategy for a period, it does not attack in equilibrium, since the defender always says "will defend." Thus, the challenger will play its equilibrium strategy as long as its expected utility from its equilibrium strategy is weakly positive, which it is for all types.

The last such strategy is to threaten and to attack if and only if the defender says "will defend." If the challenger deviates to this strategy for a period, the payoff to challengers of types $i_t^c \geq o$ is the same as if they played their equilibrium strategy, since all defenders say "will defend." As long as a solution to the system of equations exists with $o > 0$, types $i_t^c < o$ strictly prefer their equilibrium strategy to one with this payoff.

No Player Prefers to Deviate at a Node Other Than the Player's First Node in the Stage Game

To show that the equilibrium is perfect Bayesian, I also check to see that no player wishes to deviate from its equilibrium strategy restricted to the stage game at a node other than the first node of the stage game and then resume playing its equilibrium strategy in time $t + 1$. This work is straightforward and repetitive; it is available from the author upon request.

Checking that players do not want to engage in one-period deviations that begin later in the stage game results in one additional threshold, m'. The threshold m' is the cut-point between different types of defender that play one of two stage-game strategies when the defender has a reputation for honesty. The difference between the strategies played by these types occurs only off the equilibrium path; one never observes different play by these types. The equilibrium specifies that when the defender has a reputation for honesty, all defenders with types greater than m always say "will defend"; they defend if they are attacked after they have said "will defend." Thus, on the equilibrium path, defenders with types greater than m always defend if they are attacked. However, the equilibrium specifies that defenders in this situation with types between m and m' do not defend if they are attacked (off path) after they have said, "won't defend" and defenders with types between m' and 1 do defend if they are attacked after they have said "won't defend." In this eventuality (which never occurs), type m' is indifferent between defending and not defending at node h6 of figure A.1 when these actions provide the same expected utility to this type. The defender's expected utility from backing down if the challenger attacks after the defender says "won't defend" is $-i_t^d + \delta w_1$. Its expected utility from fighting is $-p i_t^d - T + \delta w_1$. Thus, a defender is indifferent when its type is m', such that $-m' + \delta w_1 = -p m' - T + \delta w_1$, or $m' = \frac{T}{1-p}$. Defenders of type $i_t^d < m'$ prefer to back down, and defenders of type $i_t^d > m'$ prefer to fight.

One can compare the off-path threshold m' to the on-path threshold m. From the previous paragraph, $m' = \frac{T}{1-p}$. From equation A.4, $m = \frac{T + \delta(w_2 - w_1)}{1-p}$. Since $w_1 > w_2$, $m < m'$. In other words, as one would expect, additional defenders back down off the equilibrium path, when they have not staked their reputation for honesty on being willing to fight if attacked.

The Impact of Communication on War and on Welfare

To evaluate the welfare effects of communication, I compare a world with communication to a hypothetical world without—that is, I compare the communicative portion of the equilibrium discussed in the text to an equilibrium in which states never can communicate (a "babbling" equilibrium). In the noncommunicative equilibrium that I consider, states play the noncommunicative strategies at the bottom of figure A.2 in every period; strategies are not history dependent, so neither player's continuation values affect its current play. This method of comparing the partially communicative equilibrium discussed in the text to the noncommunicative equilibrium contains a simplification: In the equilibrium in the text, there are some periods without communication. However, the complete payoffs in the full "communicative" equilibrium are a convex combination of the two sets of payoffs, communicative and noncommunicative, with a strictly positive weight on the communicative payoffs. Thus, the patterns I discuss later generalize immediately to the full equilibrium, though the precise numbers do not.[1] For example, if a state's average payoff is higher in the communicative part of the equilibrium that I examine than in the alternative noncommunicative equilibrium, it also is higher in the full communicative equilibrium than in the noncommunicative equilibrium. However, the difference is smaller than this thought experiment suggests.

Figure B.1 compares the probability of war with and without communication for several values of the balance of forces (p). In these examples, war is relatively cheap ($T = .2$). The figure shows a pattern: The probability of war usually is higher with communication. When the defender can communicate, it is more likely to deter an attack but it is also more prepared to fight. The probability of war is the probability that the challenger attacks a defender that tries deterrence (denoted "A") multiplied by the probability that the defender defends (denoted "D").[2] The challenger attacks under fewer circumstances when it expects the defender's

---

[1] If $X > Y$ and $Z = aX + (1 - a)Y$ where $0 < a < 1$, then $Z > Y$.

[2] Technically, the probability of war includes the probability that the challenger attacks a defender that does not try deterrence multiplied by the probability that such a defender defends, but the latter probability is always zero in this equilibrium.

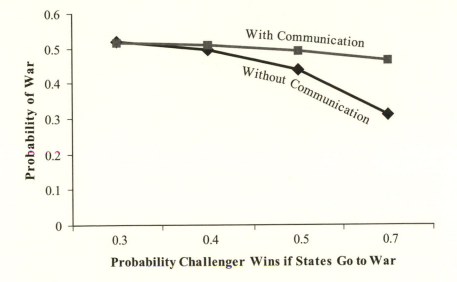

FIGURE B.1. Comparing a World with Communication to a World Without

diplomacy to be effective, so *A* is always lower with communication than without. However, the defender sometimes finds itself choosing to fight when, were it not committed, it would have chosen to back down. Thus, *D* is always higher when the defender has a reputation for honesty. The resulting probability of war (*AD*) may be either higher or lower, but usually is higher.[3]

The defender also does better, on average, when it can communicate than when it cannot. The figures do not show this fact, but figure A.2 shows why: The defender is, on average, happier with those issues that are resolved in its favor when it is able to communicate. When a defender with a reputation for honesty considers the issue to be worth less than *l* in figure A.2, it acquiesces to the challenger's demand, so these issues are never among those resolved in favor of the defender.

In this equilibrium, the ability to commit works to the defender's advantage. When the defender has not recently been caught bluffing, the defender is able to deter many attacks and its expected payoff rises sharply. The challenger's payoff, however, falls. The challenger holds an informational advantage, since the defender's value for the issues is partially revealed. However, the informational advantage comes to naught, since the information reveals that the defender is likely to defend. This

---

[3] The probability of war when the defender has a reputation for honesty is $(1-j)(1-m)$ in figure A.2. The probability when the defender has a reputation for bluffing is $(1-o)(1-q)$.

disparity between the challenger and the defender is interesting, but it probably is not a feature of the real world. In the real world, challengers almost certainly also communicate, and the average well-being of a challenger probably is higher than in this equilibrium.

Implications of the Theory

Chapter 4 tests two central implications of the theory. The chapter explains the implications from a substantive standpoint. Here, I explain why they follow from the model. I refer to the equilibrium depicted in figure A.2. Some implications of the model can be derived algebraically, such as the result on the efficacy of a threat discussed in chapter 3. However, I use the numerical solutions to find the implications that I test in chapter 4.

Implication 1. A defender with a reputation for honesty is more likely to defend following a deterrence failure than is a defender with a reputation for bluffing. In terms of the figure, $\frac{1-m}{1-l} > 1 - q$.

1. The probability that a defender with a reputation for honesty defends, conditional on the fact that it has tried to deter an attack in the first place, is $\frac{1-m}{1-l}$. (A defender with a reputation for honesty tries deterrence if its value for the issues is l or more; it defends if attacked if its value for the issues is m or more.)

2. The probability that a defender with a reputation for bluffing defends, conditional on the fact that it has tried to deter an attack in the first place, is $1 - q$. (When the defender has a reputation for bluffing, it babbles, so the probability that a defender with a reputation for bluffing defends, conditional on the fact that it has tried to deter an attack in the first place, is equal to the unconditional probability that it defends.[1] A defender defends if attacked if its value for the issues is q or more.)

3. $\frac{1-m}{1-l} > 1 - q$. (In all the equilibrium points $\{T, p, j, l, m, o, q\}$ that I find numerically, $m < q$. Since it must be that $0 < l < 1$ for the equilibrium to exist, $\frac{1-m}{1-l} > 1 - q$.)

Implication 2. A challenger is more likely to attack following the defender's attempt at deterrence when the defender has a reputation for bluffing. (The defender's attempts at deterrence are more likely to fail when it has a reputation for bluffing.) In terms of figure A.2, $(1 - j) < (1 - o)$.

---

[1] This would be the case regardless of the form of babbling.

1. The probability that the challenger attacks a defender with a reputation for honesty if the defender tries deterrence is $1 - j$.

2. The probability that the challenger attacks a defender with a reputation for bluffing is $1 - o$.

3. $j > o$ in all equilibrium points $\{T, p, j, l, m, o, q\}$ that I find, so that $(1 - j) < (1 - o)$.

The Effects of Power Status, Contiguity, and Democracy

As tables 4.4 and 4.6 report, I include several control variables in my statistical analyses to check the robustness of my results about reputations: each state's status as a major or minor power, whether or not the states are contiguous, and whether or not both states in the dyad are democratic. As I note earlier, the results about reputations are robust to the inclusion of these variables: while the estimated effects of reputations on dispute escalation change somewhat in magnitude, they remain fairly large and precise.

The estimated effects of contiguity and democracy are much as one might expect; that is, contiguous states are more likely to become involved in disputes and more likely to fight. As many previous studies find, democratic dyads are less likely to become involved in disputes and less likely to fight.[1]

The one puzzling result is about major-power status. While the term "major power" has never been well defined, many political scientists believe that major powers are more likely to have foreign policies with global range. (In fact, this claim is almost tautological, since part of the implicit conventional-wisdom definition of a major power is a state that has a foreign policy with global range.)[2] As one might expect from this conventional wisdom, challengers in my data are more likely to threaten the use of force and to escalate if either state is a major power. In addition, the defender is less likely to try deterrence if the challenger is a major power, a fact that makes some sense considering that these major-power challengers may also be more resolved. More puzzling is the fact that the defender is less likely to follow through on its threats if either state (the

---

[1] Several works question the finding of the democratic peace. I have not divided the sample as Farber and Gowa (1995) and Gowa (1999) argue that it should be divided to get accurate estimates of the effects of democracy.

[2] The commonly cited definition of a major power is from Singer and Small (1982, 45). Yet they do not really define the term. Rather, they write, "[a]lthough the criteria for differentiation between major powers and others are not as operational as we might wish, there is a high scholarly consensus on the composition of this oligarchy." This statement is quite similar to, "you know one when you see one."

challenger or itself) is a major power. Perhaps this result is due to selection effects, the precise implications of which are difficult to determine when an event has many causes—or perhaps major-power status, undefined as it is, is not a meaningful concept.

Bibliography

Abreu, D., D. Pearce, and E. Stacchetti (1986). Optimal cartel equilibria with imperfect monitoring. *Journal of Economic Theory 39*(1), 251–69.

Abreu, D., D. Pearce, and E. Stacchetti (1990). Toward a theory of discounted repeated games with imperfect monitoring. *Econometrica 58*(5), 1041–63.

Achen, C. H. (1985). Proxy variables and incorrect signs on regression coefficients. *Political Methodology 11*, 299–316.

Achen, C. H. (1986). *The Statistical Analysis of Quasi-Experiments*. Berkeley: University of California Press.

Achen, C. H. (2003). Towards a new political methodology: Microfoundations and art. *Annual Review of Political Science 5*, 423–50.

Acheson, D. (1969). *Present at the Creation*. New York: W.W. North and Company.

Albertini, L. (1952). *Origins of the War of 1914, Volume I*. London: Oxford University Press.

Alt, J. E., R. L. Calvert, and B. D. Humes (1988, June). Reputation and hegemonic stability: A game-theoretic analysis. *American Political Science Review 82*(2), 445–66.

Austen-Smith, D. (1990). Information transmission in debate. *American Journal of Political Science 34*(1), 124–52.

Austen-Smith, D. (1992). Strategic models of talk in political decision making. *International Political Science Review 13*(1), 45–58.

Axelrod, R. (1984). *The Evolution of Cooperation*. New York: Basic Books.

Axelrod, R. and W. Zimmerman (1981, April). The Soviet press on Soviet foreign policy: A usually reliable source. *British Journal of Political Science 11*, 183–200.

Barrett, G. (1950). Chou sends note. *New York Times*. August 25, p. 1.

Bennett, D. S. and A. Stam (2000). Eugene: A conceptual manual. *International Interactions 26*, 179–204.

Bradley, O. N. and C. Blair (1983). *A General's Life*. New York: Simon & Schuster.

Bremer, S. (1992). Dangerous dyads: Conditions affecting the likelihood of interstate war, 1816–1965. *Journal of Conflict Resolution 36*, 309–41.

Bueno de Mesquita, B. (1981). *The War Trap*. New Haven: Yale University Press.

Bueno de Mesquita, B. and D. Lalman (1986). Reason and war. *American Political Science Review 80*, 1113–31.

Bueno de Mesquita, B. and D. Lalman (1992). *War and Reason*. New Haven: Yale University Press.

Bueno de Mesquita, B., J. D. Morrow, and E. R. Zorick (1997, March). Capabilities, perception, and escalation. *American Political Science Review 91*, 15–27.

Chen, J. (1994). *China's Road to the Korean War.* New York: Columbia University Press.

Christensen, T. J. (1992, Summer). Threats, assurances, and the last chance for peace: The lessons of Mao's Korean War telegrams. *International Security 17,* 122–54.

Christensen, T. J. (1996). *Useful Adversaries; Grand Strategy, Domestic Mobilization, and Sino-American Conflict, 1947–1958.* Princeton: Princeton University Press.

Crawford, V. P. and J. Sobel (1982). Strategic information transmission. *Econometrica 50(6),* 1431–51.

Cumings, B. (1990). *The Origins of the Korean War; Volume II; The Roaring of the Cataract; 1947–1950.* Princeton: Princeton University Press.

de Callières, F. (1919). *The Practice of Diplomacy.* London: Constable and Company Ltd. Trans. A. F. White.

Department of State (1976a). *Foreign Relations of the United States; 1950; Volume 6; East Asia and the Pacific.* Washington, DC: U.S. Government Printing Office.

Department of State (1976b). *Foreign Relations of the United States; 1950; Volume 7; Korea.* Washington, DC: U.S. Government Printing Office.

Department of State (1996). *Foreign Relations of the United States; 1964–1968; Volume 7; Eastern Europe.* Washington, DC: U.S. Government Printing Office.

Donovan, R. J. (1982). *Tumultuous Years: The Presidency of Harry S Truman, 1949–1953.* New York: Norton.

Doyle, M. W. (1983, summer). Kant, liberal legacies, and foreign affairs. *Philosophy and Public Affairs 12(3),* 205–35.

Doyle, M. W. (1997). *Ways of War and Peace; Realism, Liberalism, and Socialism.* New York: Norton.

Dubin, J. A. and D. Rivers (1990). Selection bias in linear regression, logit and probit models. In J. Fox and J. S. Long (Eds.), *Modern Methods of Data Analysis,* pp. 410–43. Newbury Park: Sage Publications.

Esser, J. (1998). Alive and well after 25 years: A review of groupthink research. *Organizational and Behavioral and Human Decision Processes 73(2/3),* 116–41.

Farber, H. and J. Gowa (1995). Polities and peace. *International Security 20(2),* 123–46.

Farrell, J. and R. Gibbons (1989). Cheap talk can matter in bargaining. *Journal of Economic Theory 48(1),* 221–37.

Fearon, J. D. (1992). *Threats to Use Force: Costly Signals and Bargaining in International Crises.* Ph.D. thesis, University of California, Berkeley.

Fearon, J. D. (1994a, September). Domestic political audiences and the escalation of international disputes. *American Political Science Review 88(3),* 577–91.

Fearon, J. D. (1994b, June). Signaling versus the balance of power and interests: An empirical test of a crisis bargaining model. *Journal of Conflict Resolution 38,* 236–69.

Fearon, J. D. (1995, Summer). Rationalist explanations for war. *International Organization 49(3),* 379–414.

Fearon, J. D. (1997, February). Signaling foreign policy interests: Tying hands versus sinking costs. *Journal of Conflict Resolution 41*, 68–90.

Finkelstein, D. M. (1992). *Washington's Taiwan Dilemma, 1949–1950*. Fairfax, VA: George Mason University Press.

Fiske, S. T. and S. E. Taylor (1984). *Social Cognition*, chapter 4, pp. 72–91. New York: Random House.

Foot, R. (1985). *The Wrong War: American Policy and the Dimensions of the Korean Conflict, 1950–1953*. Ithaca: Cornell University Press.

Foot, R. (1991). Making known the unknown war: Policy analysis of the Korean conflict in the last decade. *Diplomatic History 15*, 411–31.

Foot, R. (1996). Leadership, perception, and interest: Chinese-American relations in the early Cold War. *Diplomatic History 20*(3), 473–82.

Freedman, L. and E. Karsh (1994). *The Gulf Conflict; 1990–1991*. Princeton: Princeton University Press.

Fudenberg, D. and J. Tirole (1992). *Game Theory*. Cambridge, MA: MIT Press.

Gaddis, J. L. (1995). *We Now Know; Rethinking Cold War History*. Oxford: Clarendon Press.

George, A. and R. Smoke (1989, January). Deterrence and foreign policy. *World Politics 41*(2), 170–82.

George, A. L. and R. Smoke (1974). *Deterrence in American Foreign Policy*. New York: Columbia University Press.

Gibbons, R. (1992). *Game Theory for Applied Economists*. Princeton: Princeton University Press.

Gochman, C. S. and Z. Maoz (1984). Militarized international disputes, 1816–1976: Procedures, patterns, and insights. *Journal of Conflict Resolution 28*(4), 585–615.

Goncharov, S. N., J. W. Lewis, and L. Xue (1993). *Uncertain Partners; Stalin, Mao, and the Korean War*. Stanford: Stanford University Press.

Gowa, J. (1999). *Ballots and Bullets*. Princeton: Princeton University Press.

Guisinger, A. and A. Smith (2002). Honest threats: The interaction of reputation and political institutions in international crises. *Journal of Conflict Resolution 46*(2), 175–200.

Halperin, M. H. (1963). *Limited War in the Nuclear Age*. New York: Wiley.

Hamilton, T. J. (1950). All Formosa solutions have their drawbacks. *New York Times*. September 3, p. 69.

Harry S Truman Presidential Oral History Collection (1990). University Publications of America. Microform.

He, D. (2003). The last campaign to unify China: The CCP's unrealized plan to liberate Taiwan, 1949–1950. In M. A. Ryan, D. M. Finkelstein, and M. A. McDevitt (Eds.), *Chinese Warfighting: The PLA Experience Since 1949*, pp. 73–90. Armonk, NY: M. E. Sharpe.

Heckman, J. J. (1974). Shadow prices, market wages, and labor supply. *Econometrica 42*, 679–94.

Heckman, J. J. (1976). The common structure of statistical models of truncation, sample selection, and limited dependent variables and a simple estimator for such models. *The Annals of Economic and Social Measurement 5*(4), 475–92.

Helmreich, E. C. (1938). *The Diplomacy of the Balkan Wars, 1912–1913*. Cambridge: Harvard University Press.

Herzig, E. (1995). *Iran and the Former Soviet South*. London: Royal Institute of International Affairs, Russian and CIS Programme.

Hopf, T. (1994). *Peripheral Visions: Deterrence Theory and American Foreign Policy in the Third World, 1965–1990*. Ann Arbor: University of Michigan Press.

Huth, P. K. (1988). *Extended Deterrence and the Prevention of War*. New Haven: Yale University Press.

Huth, P. K. (1997, Autumn). Reputations and deterrence: A theoretical and empirical assessment. *Security Studies* 7(1), 72–99.

Huth, P. K. (1998). *Standing Your Ground; Territorial Disputes and International Conflict*. Ann Arbor: University of Michigan Press.

Huth, P. K., C. Gelpi, and D. S. Bennett (1993, September). The escalation of great power militarized disputes: Testing rational deterrence theory and structural realism. *American Political Science Review* 87(3), 609–23.

Huth, P. K. and B. Russett (1984, July). What makes deterrence work? cases from 1900 to 1980. *World Politics* 36(4), 496–526.

Huth, P. K. and B. Russett (1988). Deterrence failure and crisis escalation. *International Studies Quarterly* 32, 29–46.

Huth, P. K. and B. Russett (1993, March). General deterrence between enduring rivals: Testing three competing models. *American Political Science Review* 87(1), 61–73.

Jaggers, K. and T. R. Gurr (1995, November). Tracking democracy's third wave with the Polity III data. *Journal of Peace Research* 32(4), 469–82.

Jaggers, K. and T. R. Gurr (1996). Polity III: Regime change and political authority, 1800–1994. Ann Arbor, MI: Inter-university Consortium for Political and Social Research (distributor). 2nd ICPSR ed. Boulder, CO: Keith Jaggers/College Park, MD: Ted Robert Gurr (producers), 1995.

Janis, I. L. (1983). *Groupthink: Psychological Studies of Policy Decisions and Fiascoes*. Boston: Houghton Mifflin.

Jervis, R. (1970). *The Logic of Images in International Relations*. Princeton: Princeton University Press.

Jervis, R. (1976). *Perception and Misperception in International Politics*. Princeton: Princeton University Press.

Jervis, R. (1997). *System Effects; Complexity in Political and Social Life*. Princeton: Princeton University Press.

Jones, D. M., S. A. Bremer, and J. D. Singer (1996, Fall). Militarized international disputes, 1816–1992: Rationale, coding rules, and empirical patterns. *Conflict Management and Peace Science* 15, 163–213.

Kahn, H. (1965). *On Escalation*. New York: Praeger.

Keesing's Contemporary Archives (1946). Keesing's Publishing Limited. March 2–9 and April 27–May 7.

Keesing's Contemporary Archives (1992). Keesing's Publishing Limited.

Keesing's Contemporary Archives (1993). Keesing's Publishing Limited.

Kissinger, H. (1994). *Diplomacy*. New York: Simon & Schuster.

Kreps, D. M. and R. Wilson (1982). Reputation and imperfect information. *Journal of Economic Theory* 27(2), 253–79.

Kydd, A. (2003). Which side are you on? Bias, credibility, and mediation. *American Journal of Political Science* 47(4), 597–611.

Layne, C. (1994). Kant or cant: The myth of the democratic peace. *International Security* 19, 5–49.

Lebow, R. N. (1981). *Between Peace and War*. Baltimore: Johns Hopkins University Press.

Lebow, R. N. and J. G. Stein (1990, April). Deterrence: The elusive dependent variable. *World Politics* 42(3), 336–69.

Leeds, B. A. (2004). Alliance reliability in times of war: Explaining state decisions to violate treaties. *International Organization* 57(4), 801–27.

Leng, R. J. (1993). *Interstate Crisis Behavior, 1816–1980: Realism Versus Reciprocity*. Cambridge: Cambridge University Press.

Leng, R. J. and C. S. Gochman (1984, Summer). Dangerous disputes: A study of conflict behavior and war. *American Journal of Political Science* 26(4), 664–87.

Levi, W. (1953). *Modern China's Foreign Policy*. Minneapolis: University of Minnesota Press.

Lichterman, M. (1963). To the Yalu and back. In H. Stein (Ed.), *American Civil-Military Decisions*. Birmingham: University of Alabama Press.

Lieberman, H. R. (1950a). Communist China keeps the world guessing. *New York Times*. September 3, p. 69.

Lieberman, H. R. (1950b). Peiping increases drive against U.S. *New York Times*. August 7, p. 7.

Lindsay, M. (1955). *China and the Cold War*. London: Cambridge University Press.

Maoz, Z. (1983, June). Resolve, capabilities, and the outcomes of interstate disputes. *Journal of Conflict Resolution* 27(2), 195–229.

Martin, L. (1993, April). Credibility, costs, and institutions: Cooperation on economic sanctions. *World Politics* 45(3), 406–32.

Maxwell, N. (1970). *India's China War*. London: The Trinity Press.

Maxwell, S. (1968). *Rationality in Deterrence*. London: Institute for Strategic Studies.

McKenna, J. (1962). *Diplomatic Protest in Foreign Policy*. Chicago: Loyola University Press.

Mercer, J. (1996). *Reputation and International Politics*. Ithaca: Cornell University Press.

Millett, A. R. (1997, July). A reader's guide to the Korean War. *The Journal of Military History* 61, 583–97.

Morgan, P. (1977). *Deterrence; A Conceptual Analysis*. Beverly Hills: Sage Publications.

Morgenthau, H. J. (1967). *Politics Among Nations*. New York: Alfred A. Knopf.

Morrow, J. D. (1989, November). Capabilities, uncertainty, and resolve: A limited information model of crisis bargaining. *American Political Science Review* 33(4), 941–72.

Morrow, J. D. (1994). *Game Theory for Political Scientists*. Princeton: Princeton University Press.

Munro-Leighton, J. (1992, Spring). A postrevisionist scrutiny of America's role in the Cold War in Asia, 1945–1950. *Journal of American-East Asian Relations 1*, 73–98.

Nalebuff, B. (1991). Rational deterrence in an imperfect world. *World Politics 43*(3), 313–35.

National Security Council (1968). Summary notes of the 590th meeting of the national security council. In J. E. Miller (Ed.), *Foreign Relations of the United States, 1964–1968*, Volume 17, pp. 272–8. Washington, DC: U.S. Government Printing Office.

Neustadt, R. (1990). *Presidential Power and the Modern Presidents*. New York: Free Press.

Nicolson, H. (1939). *Diplomacy*. London: Thornton Butterworth Ltd.

Orme, J. D. (1987). Deterrence failures: A second look. *International Security 11*(4), 109–12.

Paige, G. D. (1968). *The Korean Decision*. New York: Free Press.

Panikkar, K. (1955). *In Two Chinas; Memoirs of a Diplomat*. London: George Allen Unwin.

People's Daily (1950). Accomplish success and solidify (wancheng shengli, gonggu). editorial, January 1, p. 1.

People's Liberation Army Central Command (1993). Military documents on China's people's liberation war, vol. 5 (1949–6, 1950) (zhongguo renmin jiefang zhanzheng junshi wenji). Hong Kong?

Powell, R. (1990). *Nuclear Deterrence Theory*. Cambridge: Cambridge University Press.

Ramsay, K. W. (2004). Politics at the water's edge: Crisis bargaining and electoral competition. *Journal of Conflict Resolution 48*(4), 459–86.

Rees, D. (1964). *Korea: The Limited War*. London: MacMillan.

Rich, N. (1973). *Hitler's War Aims*. New York: Norton.

Ross, L. and C. A. Anderson (1982). Shortcomings in the attribution process: On the origins and maintenance of erroneous social assessments. In D. Kahneman, P. Slovic, and A. Tversky (Eds.), *Judgement Under Uncertainty: Heuristics and Biases*, pp. 129–52. Cambridge: Cambridge University Press.

Rousseau, D. L., C. Gelpi, D. Reiter, and P. K. Huth (1996, September). Assessing the dyadic nature of the democratic peace, 1918–88. *American Political Science Review 90*(3), 512–33.

Rovere, R. H. (1950). Letter from Washington. *The New Yorker*, 52–4. September 2 issue, August 25 submission date.

Rovere, R. H. and A. M. Schlesinger, Jr. (1951). *The General and the President*. New York: Farrar, Straus and Young.

Russett, B. (1963). The calculus of deterrence. *Journal of Conflict Resolution 7*(2), 97–109.

Russett, B. (1993). *Grasping the Democratic Peace*. Princeton: Princeton University Press.

Sartori, A. E. (2001, April). Hawks, doves, and diplomats; reputation and communication in a modified hawk-dove game. Unpublished manuscript.

Sartori, A. E. (2002). The might of the pen; a reputational theory of communication in international disputes. *International Organization* 56(1), 121–49.

Sartori, A. E. (2003). An estimator for some binary-outcome selection models without exclusion restrictions. *Political Analysis* 11(2), 111–38.

Schelling, T. C. (1960). *The Strategy of Conflict.* Cambridge: Harvard University Press.

Schelling, T. C. (1966). *Arms and Influence.* New Haven: Yale University Press.

Schnabel, J. F. (1992). *Policy and Direction; The First Year.* Washington, DC: U.S. Government Printing Office.

Schnabel, J. F. and R. J. Watson (1979). *The History of the Joint Chiefs of Staff; Volume 2; The Korean War.* Wilmington, DE: Michael Glazier.

Schultz, K. (1998). Domestic opposition and signaling in international crises. *American Political Science Review* 92(4), 829–44.

Schultz, K. (2001). *Democracy and Coercive Diplomacy.* Cambridge: Cambridge University Press.

Silber, L. and A. Little (1997). *Yugoslavia; Death of a Nation.* New York: Penguin Books.

Singer, J., S. Bremer, and J. Stuckey (1972). Capability distribution, uncertainty, and major power war, 1820–1965. In B. Russett (Ed.), *Peace, War and Numbers.* Beverly Hills: Sage Publications.

Singer, J. D. and M. Small (1982). *Resort to Arms; International and Civil Wars; 1816–1980.* Beverly Hills: Sage Publications.

Siverson, R. M. and H. Starr (1990). Opportunity, willingness, and the diffusion of war. *American Political Science Review* 84(1), 47–67.

Smith, A. (1998a). The effect of foreign policy statements on foreign nations and domestic electorates. In R. M. Siverson (Ed.), *Strategic Politicians, Institutions and Foreign Policy.* Ann Arbor: University of Michigan Press.

Smith, A. (1998b). International crises and domestic politics. *American Political Science Review* 92(3), 623–38.

Snyder, G. H. (1961). *Deterrence and Defense.* Princeton: Princeton University Press.

Snyder, G. H. and P. Diesing (1977). *Conflict Among Nations.* Princeton: Princeton University Press.

Spence, A. M. (1974). *Market Signalling.* Cambridge: Harvard University Press.

Stacchetti, E. (1994). Infinitely repeated games. From Economics 755, University of Michigan.

Stearns, M. (1996). *Talking to Strangers; Improving American Diplomacy at Home and Abroad.* Princeton: Princeton University Press.

Stueck, W. (1995). *The Korean War; An International History.* Princeton: Princeton University Press.

Stueck, W. (2002). *Rethinking the Korean War.* Princeton: Princeton University Press.

't Hart, P. (1991). Irving L. Janis' victims of groupthink. *Political Psychology* 12(2), 247–78.

Tang, Y. and G. Xu (2001). *The Study of Important CCP Historical Events (zhongguo gongchandang zhongda shishi kaozheng).* Beijing: Chinese Documentary Publisher.

Truman, H. S. (1956). *Memoirs; Volume Two; Years of Trial and Hope.* Garden City, NY: Doubleday.

Turner, L. (1970). *Origins of the First World War.* New York: Norton.

Twomey, C. (2004). *The Military Lens: Doctrinal Differences, Misperception, and Deterrence Failure in Sino-American Relations.* Ph.D. thesis, Massachusetts Institute of Technology.

United States Congress Senate (1951). Military situation in the Far East; hearings before the Committee on Armed Services and the Committee on Foreign Relations. Washington, DC: U.S. Government Printing Office. Eighty-Second Congress, First Session, Part I, May 3, 1951.

Van de Ven, W. P. and B. Van Praag (1981). The demand for deductibles in private health insurance. *Journal of Econometrics 17,* 229–52.

Vasquez, J. A. (1998). *The Power of Power Politics: From Classical Realism to Neotraditionalism.* Cambridge: Cambridge University Press.

Weede, E. (1976). Overwhelming preponderance as a pacifying condition among contiguous Asian dyads. *Journal of Conflict Resolution 20,* 395–412.

Whiting, A. S. (1960). *China Crosses the Yalu.* New York: Macmillan.

Wilson, R. (1985). Reputations in games and markets. In A. E. Roth (Ed.), *Game-Theoretic Models of Bargaining,* pp. 27–61. Cambridge: Cambridge University Press.

Wu, S. (1990). To attack or not to attack. *Journal of Conflict Resolution 34,* 531–52.

Zelman, W. A. (1967). Chinese intervention in the Korean War: A bilateral failure of deterrence. Technical report, University of California, Los Angeles. Security Studies Paper 11.

Zhang, S. and J. Chen (1996). *Chinese Communist Foreign Policy and the Cold War in Asia; Documentary Evidence, 1944–1950.* Chicago: Imprint Publications.

Index

Page numbers in *italics* refer to figures or tables in the text.